EX LIBRIS

VINTAGE CLASSICS

THE ART OF LOVE

Publius Ovidius Naso was born in Italy on 20 March 43 BC. He was educated in Rome and worked as a public official before taking up poetry full-time. His earliest surviving work is the collection of love poems called the *Amores*, which was followed by the *Heroides*. The *Ars Amatoria* (*The Art of Love*) and the *Remedia Amoris* (*The Cure for Love*) were probably written between 2 BC and AD 2. These were followed by his two epic poems the *Fasti* and the *Metamorphoses*. In AD 8 Ovid fell out of favour with the Emperor Augustus due to a '*carmen et error*' ('a poem and a mistake') and was banished to what is now Romania. While in exile he wrote *Tristia, Ibis* and the *Epistulae ex Ponto* which consists of letters appealing for help in his efforts to be recalled to Rome. Ovid died in exile in AD 18.

Tom Payne was born in 1971. He read Classics at Corpus Christi College, Cambridge. For four years he was deputy literary editor of the *Daily Telegraph*. He lives with his wife and four children in Dorset, and teaches English and Classics at Sherborne School. He is the author of *Fame*, published by Vintage Originals.

OVID

The Art of Love

with The Cures for Love
and Treatments for the Feminine Face

TRANSLATED, ANNOTATED AND INTRODUCED BY
Tom Payne

WITH A FOREWORD BY
Hephzibah Anderson

VINTAGE BOOKS
London

Published by Vintage 2012

2 4 6 8 10 9 7 5 3 1

Translation, introduction and notes © Tom Payne 2011
Foreword © Hephzibah Anderson 2011

Vintage
Random House, 20 Vauxhall Bridge Road,
London SW1V 2SA

www.vintage-classics.info

Addresses for companies within The Random House Group Limited
can be found at: www.randomhouse.co.uk/offices.htm

The Random House Group Limited Reg. No. 954009

A CIP catalogue record for this book
is available from the British Library

ISBN 9780099518822

The Random House Group Limited supports The Forest Stewardship
Council (FSC®), the leading international forest certification
organisation. Our books carrying the FSC label are printed on
FSC® certified paper. FSC is the only forest certification scheme
endorsed by the leading environmental organisations, including
Greenpeace. Our paper procurement policy can be found at
www.randomhouse.co.uk/environment

Typeset in Dante MT by Palimpsest Book Production Limited,
Falkirk, Stirlingshire
Printed and bound by CPI Group (UK) Ltd, Croydon, CR0 4YY

CONTENTS

FOREWORD

Pity the poor poet. With nothing more than his verse to offer, he's destined to be ever unlucky when it comes to wooing the ladies – poetry may win praise, but it'll never be enough to get the girl. So sighs Ovid midway through his mock-didactic *The Art of Love*. He's being coyly disingenuous, of course. By the time he turned 30, the Roman author had not only staked his claim as a doyen of the erotic elegy, he was also twice divorced and thrice married.

In these nimble new translations of works written in his prime, saucy asides depict Ovid as a poet and a player both. He's the guy who'll talk a girl's phone number from her even as she rolls her eyes at his dog-eared lines. He does something similar with the reader, too – that practised self-deprecation? It's just a part of the act, along with jokes at his own expense and ironic mockery of the man in the mirror. One way or another, he will win you over.

At first glance, *The Art of Love* appears to be a his-and-hers seduction primer. A triptych, its opening two books are intended for male eyes only. 'Concentrate, men, even if you're morons,' he orders, going on to tell them how to find love, and how to hold on to it. He advises on places to meet women, on chat-up lines and smooth moves. Make her feel special, he prompts. Flatter her. Become her confidant, her handyman, her slave – literally. Do not, under any circumstances, take no for an answer.

Timing is crucial – look for a moment when your rivals are in her bad books. He has warnings to impart as well. Beware the impact that booze and low lighting can have on your judgement. Don't over-groom, he reminds Rome's metrosexuals; do get a decent haircut, but there's no need to go pumicing those hairy legs.

To make an erotic conquest requires a bit of luck; retaining it, he notes, takes cunning. He's at the ready with suggestions sly and plentiful here, too. Agree with her, laugh with her, notice her outfit and tell her how beautiful she looks. Lie, if you must. His advice extends to the bedroom, where a man should pretend that the object of his affections is doing everything right – even when she's not.

Though he favours the sporting metaphor, it isn't merely for the sake of levelling the playing field that this work's third book is for women. For Ovid, his paramour must enjoy – or at least appear to enjoy – sex as much as he does. 'I hate sex when it brings uneven joys,' he huffs. And if he goes on to devote substantially more attention to telling women how to fake an orgasm than how attain one – well, it's not as if he hasn't already advised men to do the same.

You'll find scant sense on these pages of the sexes hailing from different planets. Indeed, much of Ovid's advice is interchangeable. If not, it's reversible. Having told men never to accept no as a final answer, what does he tell women? Say no. Or at least delay and rebuff. Yet book three is less about enabling women to wise up and protect themselves against wily men than giving them the tools to go out and make conquests of their own. 'Look after looks,' he counsels. Don't overdo it when it comes to getting dressed up – makeup is your friend, but never let a man see you applying it. Eat and drink daintily, learn to sing and watch your posture. Remember: accentuate the positive.

With the exception of some of his *Treatments for the Feminine Face* (kingfisher cream, anyone?), there's little here that cannot be transposed to the 21st century dating dilemma. You wrote to your girl and haven't heard back? 'Send her more things to read, and make them slushy.' Whether the medium is a wax tablet or a text, its message remains the same.

Plenty of Ovid's advice has a familiar ring to it. You'll have heard – perhaps even hummed – it before: it's the tried-and-tested wisdom of rock ballads and country standards. Treat 'em mean to keep 'em keen. Unless you want to lose a lover, don't go bragging about them to your friend, lest they think they're missing something. The pace of courtship may change, but its dynamics remain constant. Cads will eternally 'seek fame from a shag', and there will always be women who 'reject what's here, and love what goes', mooning after Mr Unavailable. It's uncanny to find that Ovid, from so many centuries distant, is so thoroughly on to we moderns.

But for all its similarities, Ovid's world is not ours. Though his shoulder-shrugging 'not for me' ease with homosexuality suggests we've plenty in common, his readiness to list physical force as an amatory aid jars. The women he was addressing would have been a particular kind – courtesans, essentially – while Augustus' Julian Marriage Laws had made a serious crime of adultery, lending danger to the poet's barely concealed allusions to extra-marital trysts.

In 8 AD Ovid was exiled to Tomis on the Black Sea. He would never make it home. Though *The Art of Love* is generally believed to have been written half-a-dozen years before his banishment, some scholars nevertheless hold its skimpily veiled libertinism responsible. More likely, he became inadvertently caught up in someone else's scandal or plot, and the poem simply provided a handy pretext, but it's a sharp reminder of the steep cost that love can exact.

When Ovid talks of love, he's referring to a hybrid of the romantic and the lusty. Splitting the heart from the body, today's pop culture tends to neuter love, glossing it with Hallmark platitudes or else airbrushing it with caricatured raunch. Ovid's *amor* is fierce. Unruly, chaotic and all-consuming, it's as often a curse as a blessing, and definitely not something to be contained within bullet-pointed tips and how-tos. Once Cupid has you in his crosshairs, there is very little you can do. Ovid trained as a lawyer, and must have taken particular delight in sketching that scene in *The Art of Love* when Venus 'hoots' to see how defenceless the slick-talking guys down at the law courts are before Cupid's arrows.

Ovid appreciated something that today's self-declared pickup artists are staunchly in denial of: our individual uniqueness. And thus, however informative, the didactic poem – or the seduction manual, for that matter – can ultimately assist only so much. This is especially true between the sheets. As he puts it, 'there's no position that will do / for everyone; find one that's right for you'.

There's a teenage kick to be had from finding a bona fide pillar of the rhetorical tradition advising on sexual positions, but

Ovid's uninhibited use of the word love – that yields a still greater frisson. Just as women once put off putting out, so we all – men and women both – tiptoe around the L-word nowadays, skittish as Victorian virgins. We're far more comfortable talking about sex, though our close-up focus on technique – on sex as a kind of erotic workout – has resulted in guides that are about as personal as instructions for knocking up a flat-pack futon. Coupled with our passion for using evolutionary biology to explain away the mysteries of desire, we risk losing sight of a vital – and thrillingly sensual – human dimension. Cynical though they may sound, Ovid's apercus come with a recurring caveat: to be loved, you have to project something of yourself from within – 'a pretty face isn't enough.'

Ovid knows that his subject and form are essentially incompatible, and it's this stormy friction that makes the poems so intensely pleasurable. We all have moments of self-doubt when heartache nudges us towards the self-help shelves and books that seem to offer the solutions to our romantic woes. Some of us go so far as to write them. And yet deep down, we know that there can be no real protection against love. Ovid jokes about it. He is risqué and ribald and knowing. But even as he satirises the form, he celebrates his subject – untameable, unpredictable, uncontrollable love, a force far beyond the power of an instructional elegy.

In *The Cures for Love*, he adopts the tone of a doctor. Still, he cannot pretend that his prescription will inoculate you against a relapse. For instance, to get over love, you might retreat to the country and become a farmer. Reasonable enough advice, except that within a few lines, Ovid has seduced himself away from his own purpose with fecund imagery of ripening crops and plump grapes ready to be crushed between bare toes. Hardly what a recovering victim of *amor* wants to hear.

These digressions have a will of their own. From mythology, he plucks cautionary tales of love gone awry – Pasiphae, who fell for a bull, or Procris, who realised too late that her lover's adulterous-sounding words were addressed merely to the breeze. None of these stories ends well, but they're so good, it's hard not to feel thankful that their misled protagonists were human enough to fall head over heels. 'Avoid affairs at all if you want happy ends', is Ovid's terse moral, but he knows that without the love drug, there'd be nothing to tell.

And so, as he parodies romantic poetry, hamming up the misery of those enslaved to love and sending up the notion of love as a malady, he simultaneously bows down before Venus. His verse serves as a reminder that while passion can make a fool of the best of us, it needn't rob us of our eloquence. Rhetoric may not be much of a shield when Cupid takes aim, but longing and desire – these eternal subjects are worthy of our keenest wits. Tom Payne's spirited translation captures all the mischief and magnifi-cence of Ovid's voice, vaulting him into the twenty-first century to reclaim love from the fluffy realms of pink-jacketed sagas and relationship quackery.

Hephzibah Anderson, 2010

INTRODUCTION

I. NOW AND THEN

How to conceal curves; how to exploit your girlfriend's suspicions; how to make the most of her illness; the best way to describe her appearance without causing offence; how to hide stretch marks when you're making out; how to stay beautiful when losing a board game; discreet ways of making out during public entertainments: the appeal to us today of Ovid's guidebook on love is manifold. The irony is that Ovid achieved this lasting relevance by burying himself in the realities of a vastly different sphere, the Rome of Augustus Caesar. What makes him so modern turns out to be his attention to that ancient world of his.

We could add erectile dysfunction to a list of Ovid's concerns, and abortion; there's advice on diet, too, and that fine line between looking well-groomed and looking effeminate. The first two concerns appear in an earlier collection of poems, the *Amores*;[1] the others bounce from the pages below. *The Art of Love* sometimes surprises us because it offers advice we could actually use, or else adapt without too much difficulty to suit our own circumstances. It's almost a shock that our worlds should touch on so many points.

As we shall see, though, it's just when we feel safest that Ovid surprises us with something we'd baulk at. For example, Roman elegists seem clear that a certain amount of domestic force, *vis*, is acceptable. Tibullus identifies hair-pulling as fine, and hitting as not fine. Ovid works within these parameters, although he is clearly embarrassed about it. Even so, in *The Art of Love* he expatiates on the rape of the Sabine women, a story key to the Romans' sense of how they came to be who they are, with a mixture of opprobrium and smirking. For important reasons, to do with both custom and law, Ovid lived somewhere utterly foreign.

This is reflected in both the content and style of *The Art of Love*. It is a work that has caused offence throughout the ages, in part because earlier readers have feared that smut lies within its scrolls. When Ovid was exiled from Rome, he blamed not only a political mistake he'd made, but also this poem.[2] He blamed the poem, although the error was the more likely reason (*The Art of Love* had been available for perhaps six years by the time the emperor exiled him). And if the poem did have anything to do with Ovid's fall from grace, we can be confident that this was not so much because it was pornographic, as because the poet's irony did too little to conceal the ridicule that he felt Augustus' laws on adultery deserved.

It fits more with our view of history to find that later ages did indeed find against the poem for a surfeit of smut. Here, for example, is some of the special pleading Dryden and his publisher felt necessary before putting out the work:

They [the three books] are very far from being so licentious as the Writings of several other Poets, both *Greek* and *Latin*. However we must own he might have been a little more discreet, especially in some Places . . .

As for this Treatise of the *Art of Love,* for which the Author has also prescrib'd a *Remedy,* as it is liable to be ill interpreted by those whose Pens poison every Thing they touch; so it may bear a good Construction, by such as know how to turn every Thing to Advantage.

I will say, this *Art* may be apply'd to those that intend to marry. There is nothing sure against Decency in all that. I agree, if you will have it so, that it extends so far as to direct one to the Means to gain a Mistress. If this was not lawful heretofore in *Italy,* on account of the jealous Humour of the *Italians,* we cannot, for the same Reason only, say it ought to be forbidden in our Country, any more than in several others, provided we could be sure the Ladies Modesty would not be offended, before whom Youth should be always careful not to exceed the Bounds of the Respect that's due to them.

This tells us much about Dryden's time, and something of Ovid's, too. If Dryden wanted to be rude in his writing, he could, so long as he deployed some ambiguity (a song from *Marriage à la Mode* has him use the word 'die' a lot, for example). The surest way to present erotic literature to readers was to pass it off as something worthy and classical, and Dryden managed this more suggestively when translating Lucretius than when rendering Ovid. Even so, Dryden omits the passage at the end of Book 3 that catalogues the sexual positions that women can adopt to flatter their figures.

Dryden's preface takes us straight to one of the biggest surprises readers face: that *The Art of Love* is less a *Kama Sutra,* and more a self-help guide, constructed with a self-knowing wit and panache that we don't find so readily in *The Rules* or *Men Are from Mars, Women Are from Venus*. Dryden is right, too, to suggest that Ovid's advice is as useful to the married man or woman as it is to the unattached. The plan of the work as a whole reflects this: Book 1 is about where to find women, and how to woo them. Book 2 is about how to make a relationship last. Book 3 offers advice for women.

However useful all this is, one of the best sustained jokes in *The Art of Love* is about the effectiveness of any literary guidance. Ovid is quick to point out that, although other poets have written didactic, instructive books on other subjects, he is different: unlike Hesiod, for example, he is not relying on a muse, or on Apollo, but on his own experience. So right from the start, he is presenting himself both as an authority and as a love poet, who seeks fame from his own sufferings, and who nobly offers himself to us so that we can lead better (love) lives.

It's just as well that he uses his own experience, and regularly encourages us to manipulate our own strengths, as well as to downplay our weaknesses. It subverts the relationship between lecturer and audience, so that we can bring something of ourselves to the lesson. But, as commentators commonly observe about didactic literature, it's more about the literature than the teaching. No farmer would trust Virgil's *Georgics* more than his own understanding of the land he works. No one bitten by a snake is likely to have Nicander's handy book on the subject in his or her backpack. Similarly, a steadfast reliance on Ovid's pulling techniques is as likely to land you in trouble as in bed. A discriminating reading, though, might be more successful. For this reason, it's worth stating that neither the author nor the publisher bears responsibility for any damage the reader may incur by following the advice below, nor for any loss, of lover or of face.

Still, read *The Art of Love* and you start to find its precepts everywhere – on television, in agony columns, in magazines in the dentist's waiting room. How to make the most of your smile. Why candles at a dinner party are important. When to go shopping without the risk of spending too much. (When they're shut, is the bloody-minded answer; but bear in mind that this advice is aimed at men.)

So, given that this is a book that raised eyebrows in Ovid's lifetime, was burnt in Savonarola's Bonfire of the Vanities in 1497, added to the Vatican's index of books you shouldn't read in 1564, and confiscated by US Customs between 1926 and 1930, modern readers might be more disappointed by how little sex there is in *The Art of Love*, rather than by how much. By 1971, he could safely be taught in schools, in portions judiciously selected by M. J. Griggs.[3]

It is true that Ovid is less rude than Catullus, Juvenal or Martial, but there's a simple reason for this. He's happier. Take the example of the Lucretius that Dryden brought to such life in 1685:

> Nor when the Youthful pair more closely joyn,
> When hands in hands they lock, and thighs in
>   thighs they twine
> Just in the raging foam of full desire,
> When both press on, both murmur, both expire,
> They grip, they squeeze, their humid tongues they
>   dart,
> As each would force their way to t'other's heart:

This is so fruity because it is ultimately fruitless – it is

> In vain; they only cruze about the coast,
> For bodies cannot pierce, nor be in bodies lost.

Lucretius' argument is a subtle one, deriving from Epicurus, that sex stimulates the desire for more sex, and so is never going to be wholly fulfilling. Ovid, on the other hand, starts from the position that sex is so good that it is beyond words, and that, in any case, if you know how good it is, you don't need elegiac couplets to take the place of coupling. After a love poem devoted to the setting of a tryst, Ovid withholds an account of the sex itself: *cetera quis nescit?* he writes – who doesn't know the rest? Similarly, the presumption of *The Art of Love* is, if you're reading this because you want sex, you already know that it's worth it.

It's revealing, then, that on those few occasions when Ovid does describe congress, it's either when he's advising women, or else when he's considering a woman's pleasure. He talks about orgasms really to assert that women should enjoy them too; he explains that one reason why he prefers sex with women to sex with men is that he prefers orgasms to be simultaneous; and he says that neither party should overtake the other in a race to the climax. This doesn't save him from the charge of privileging a man's pleasure over a woman's: the man has two books devoted to his craft, after all, while the woman has just the one;[4] and it's clear that the woman's pleasure is at least part of the man's (Ovid says firmly that a woman should fake for this reason). But, at least when he is compared to other elegists, or to Lucretius, Ovid's exuberance manages to be tactful, even tasteful.

II. THEN

Given how readily some of Ovid's advice commends itself to different generations, it is sometimes tempting to translate and update at the same time. I've resisted this temptation for a number of reasons. One reason is shown by a glance at Henry Fielding's prose translation of Book 1, published in 1759 (five years after his death). Sometimes it works –

> Beauties are as plenty in the City of *London* as Apples in *Herefordshire*, or Grains of Wheat in Hampshire.

– and sometimes it doesn't:

> *Pasiphae*, I am very sorry to say it, conceived a Passion worse, if possible, than that of Mrs *Mary Hamilton*, for this Bull. Lady —— is not more envied in the Drawing-Room than was every handsome heifer by this unfortunate Woman.[5]

or

> Mr *Miller* will tell you, that the same kind of Soil is not proper to all Fruits.

So will Bunny Guinness, and Diarmuid Gavin, but will we know about them in 250 years' time? The biggest danger is to give the impression that Ovid is writing with a modern lack of constraint, or with twenty-first-century sensibilities. But however fair he appeared to be to women, and however progressive in his urging that men be attentive to them, his culture was different, and, more immediately, so was the law. The law will give us an insight into that culture, especially since it had changed so dramatically, and so recently.

In 18 BC, Augustus legislated against adultery. If a man had sex with another man's wife, both parties were banished to different islands. Cuckolds could, in theory, kill their wives' lovers; fathers could kill both their daughters and their daughters' lovers. A man could have sex out of wedlock so long as it was with an unmarried woman, a slave or a prostitute. Prostitution was legal, so long as prostitutes declared themselves as such. It was even possible to register as a prostitute in order to escape punishment as an adulterer.

All this is a problem for Ovid. He is the master of erotic elegy. His *Amores* are littered with smart ways of cheating, and how to elude his girlfriend's *vir* (man, a word that can mean husband, but needn't). There's not much he can do about this. In the *Amores* he adopts a number of ploys to show how he can't help writing love elegy;[6] and once you've decided to write poetry in the genre of Tibullus, Propertius and Gallus, you are exploring a world in which there's no mention of your beloved being your spouse, and where there is frequent mention of infidelity. It was a standard joke, as obvious in its way as Byron's quip, 'Think you, if Laura had been Petrarch's wife, / He would have written sonnets all his life?'[7] And it was a joke Ovid's forerunners had in turn inherited from the Roman comedies of Plautus, who inherited it from the Greek comedies of Menander. *The Art of Love* uses a reference to the theatre to hint at adultery, as though Ovid is trying to defend a Roman convention:

applaud the mime who plays the woman's part;
favour the third party who wins her heart.[8]

Ovid's first published elegies date to about 25 BC, when he
was 18. So he had been immersed in the form for a while before
18 BC. His *Amores* appeared two years after the adultery law, and
he seems to have come to no harm for this. But in *The Art of
Love*, there is a significant change. At several points he spells out,
as if for the security camera, exactly who is legally cleared to
read his book:

No matron's bands. No signs of modesty.
No skirts with hems much lower than the knee.[9]

It's safe and customary to cheat on friends;
customary, but a criminal offence.[10]

If these things [signs of cheating] are worth
    catching, catch them when
water and fire have made you married men.
No dames in long skirts: as I've said before,
let's keep to fun permitted by the law.[11]

So learn my precepts, girls, while I've the wit –
if modesty, or laws, or rights, permit.[12]

Now, you're not married. Even so, deploy
a trick that's guaranteed to fool a boy.[13]

As a way of dodging the censor, this could be subtler. The biggest problem he has, especially when he offers advice to women, is to pretend that he doesn't want married women to read the book. Which leaves him with unmarried women, slaves or prostitutes. To write for the first category would be corrupting; for the second, an unlikely kindness; for the third, otiose.[14] Ovid does manage to talk about extra-marital sex under the guise of a possible loophole in this: the freedwoman. Whether he was allowed to do this is debatable.[15]

There is a further possibility – that really, he's writing for men all along. But he does entertain the idea that women read poems (which don't make such bad gifts). The question remains, what type of woman? The recent law made the cat-egorisation of women all the more rigid, and a matter of forensic wrangling. These categories were identifiable by their clothes: the *matron* wore a *stola*, which Kelly Olson describes as 'a slip-like garment with over-the-shoulder straps, worn over the tunic and reaching to the ground, and belted under the breast with a plain cord'[16] They would also wear *vittae* – woollen bands in the hair. Prostitutes wore a toga, although some are described as naked, which could be taken to mean topless. Mistaking these two categories was undesirable, but possible. It was an offence to proposition a matron in a public place, unless the man could prove that this was an understandable mistake.[17] An epigram of Martial's shows us how he puts his options into leagues:

I'd like a girl born free. If she says no,
then to a freedwoman is where I go.

Last is a slave; but she's best of the three
if her face makes her look like someone free.[18]

Ovid's challenge is to negotiate these niceties without sounding
as though he's writing a guidebook for whores. As Roy Gibson
shows, introducing his commentary to Book 3, the result is a
mishmash: Ovid did write a poem[19] in which he overhears a
madame (a *lena*) giving advice to a trainee. But in *The Art of Love*,
Book 3 he ends up in the role both of Apollonian authority and
also of the brothel-keeper he so despised before. He must juggle
some kind of empowerment for women with his own male interests. And those male interests, not as questioned or challenged
in Augustan Rome as they are now, do much to account for what
in Ovid seems remote to us now. The results of this hedging can
be entertaining or hypocritical, or, if the latter is conscious, both.

III. WHERE'S OVID?

The debate about how much we need to know about a writer's
life is an especially vexed one with Ovid, because a lot of information is available. We can work backwards, with an extreme
example: to read his *Tristia*, his poems from exile, we need to
know that he really was in exile; and then, it becomes hard not
to make something of his veiled references to how he ended up
there. As we have seen, he blames a poem (a *carmen*, presumably *The Art of Love*) and an *error*.

Ovid was exiled in AD 8. He was sent to the town of
Tomis, in what is now Rumania, by the Black Sea. Although
we know exactly when he was born (March 20, 43 BC), we

don't know the date of his death; 17 AD seems likely. He never came back to Rome. Although there has been much speculation about a line in the *Tristia* – 'Why did I see what I saw? Why did I contaminate my eyes?'[20] – we don't know what he saw. It's tempting to speculate that he knew something about Augustus' daughter Julia that Augustus didn't know; Julia was banished for adultery in AD 2, a likely publication date of *The Art of Love*. The names, dates and places of the scandal are as reliable as any gossip is – five named men, including Mark Antony's son, and something to do with the speaker's rostrum. And Ovid's *carmen* appeared at the same time as these *errores*.

If the *carmen* itself was an *error*, then we have seen some examples above of the net-curtains he hung to conceal it, but it's hard to find specific faults. There are moments when one feels that Augustus might have taken exception to the tone, or found the whole enterprise shameful. Ovid's love of sophistication, and scorn of simplicity, might be part of the problem. There's nothing immediately wrong with his thoughts on *cultus*, for example, at the beginning of Book 3, and a brief, right-on rant about showy building projects of the rich that extend out into the sea could well have rung true to Augustus, whose own accommodation on the Palatine was more Downing Street than White House. But flings, secret notes tucked down bras, women tippling and bribing chaperones, men groping them at the races – these weren't part of the Rome Augustus wanted his poets to commemorate.

One other vital fact about Ovid's life can provide his defence: he was a lawyer. In the *Amores* he wrote that he didn't 'prostitute his voice' in the forum, but we're in no doubt that he could have done. That use of 'prostitute' is more than another sex reference; it's used in the way that Holden Caulfield uses it when he calls his brother one for going to Hollywood. Lawyers were banned from taking fees. It was a running joke that they became rich through baksheesh. Ovid was of the equestrian class – he was a knight – and so this would have been *infra dignitatem*. And anyway, as he often wrote, he was a poet, and wanted a more lasting fame.

Still, in the *Tristia*, he pleads to Augustus that he defended his clients when asked; and Ovid in court would make for good legal drama. As a law student, he became skilled in the art of the *controversia*, an exercise to develop the facility of arguing a case from both sides. Lawyers (then as now) could impress their peers by advancing apparently lost causes. Seneca remembers Ovid defending youthful passion over elderly restraint.[21] The best lost cause ever was Helen of Troy: a glance at Aeschylus' *Agamemnon* shows what disgusted rhetoric her very name inspired. When Gorgias the sophist was touting for business in Athens, he would launch into her defence. Here is Ovid on the subject:

When Menelaus goes, who takes his place?
Helen accepts her guest's tepid embrace.
You left them, Menelaus – you're the goof
whose wife and guest were under the same roof.
You'd give a hawk some timid doves to keep
or leave a wolf on mountains full of sheep.
It wasn't Helen's error, or the man's –
he did what you'd have done, given the chance.
You gave adultery a time and place;

Paris did Helen only by your grace.
Her bed was solitary; she was distressed
and then in came a reconstructed guest.
A gentleman had her. What could she do?
She is absolved. Menelaus, I blame you.[22]

The poet is showing off. He'd practised this skill, not only at law school, but also when writing his *Heroides* – the letters of the heroines, in which wronged women spoke, or wrote, their sides of the story. Helen (who doesn't appear in the *Heroides*) is the benchmark of versatility, and it's an attribute that Ovid deploys throughout *The Art of Love*. It explains why he can urge men to do something, and then urge women to do either the same thing, or something quite different. Should men renege on promises? Absolutely. Should women? Never. Is lisping sweet? Sometimes, sometimes not. Should you conceal affairs? Yes. And also, no. In this last case, Ovid is quite open about his flip from one argument to its opposite:

Just now I urged discretion; still, sometimes
change tack: I say, reveal your secret crimes.
Don't knock this inconsistency: one breeze
alone won't take a crew across the seas.

Even the defence for being unconvincing is convincing. The legal training can go so far as to explain the very existence of *The Cures for Love*. Here he takes on Cupid, that rude boy who needed controlling in *The Art of Love*, and says that he has become more savage than he should be. Ovid delivers a speech that even the love god must accept. The rest is more *controversia*: he urges readers to unlearn the things they learnt before. Before, for example, he urged girls with bad teeth not to smile. In the *Cures*, he says that a man who wants to get over a girl with, say, bad teeth should make her laugh.

IV. TASTE

Given all this legal dexterity, it's harder to see why he was caught out by the events of 2 AD, or 8 AD, or anything in between. It's perfectly possible that the sentence handed down to a lesser wit for whatever it was that Ovid did and/or didn't do would have been death. But, as I have suggested, the banishment is as likely to be one of taste, and if so, then that of Augustus wasn't for disputing.

This, too, is a kind of irony. Throughout the poem, Ovid tries so hard to present an elegant balance. He's at his satirical best when he's attacking the extremes of his age: men who take too much care over their appearance; men who are likely to raid their girlfriends' wardrobes; women whose couture might outdo Victoria Beckham at one end and Vicky Pollard at the other:

> One girl sashays with skill; her tunic flows,
> catching the breeze; she proudly points her toes,
> whereas an Umbrian wife, whose cheeks are red,
> ambles bow-legged with a mighty tread.
> As ever, let there be a middle way:
> one is a peasant, and the other's fay.[23]

This love of balance is conventional enough: the words 'nothing to excess' (*meden agan*) were inscribed at the temple of Apollo at Delphi, alongside the words 'know yourself' (*gnothi seauton*), which Ovid discusses[24] in his poem. The problem is that Ovid does know himself, and while he expresses himself with an astounding elegance, it's the scale on which he lays out his ideas that pushes the envelope. As L. P. Wilkinson concludes, 'The case against Ovid rested on degree; the *Ars Amatoria* was in a class by itself, because of its exclusive and expressed intention, its scope and its shamelessness.'[25] Ovid's style can be epigrammatic and condensed; but having established that he's going to write a treatise on how to attract people and seduce them – his expressed intention – then his scope becomes extensive. Critics have often complained that Ovid doesn't let a good idea go. This is another reason why we have *The Cures for Love* alongside the *Art*; and why, by the way, his *Metamorphoses* is at once brilliant and baggy.

The structure of *The Art of Love* admits many digressions, forced links, mythological *exempla* and inversions of advice previously given. Here, though, it is part of his irrepressible brio – if the cautious old man he cited in his student *controversia* is saying 'down, boy' to his younger self, the lusty pup isn't listening. And in any case, this way of rambling and improvising befits the subject.

V STYLE

But how is it possible to be epigrammatic and exhaustive? The answer is in Ovid's metre, the elegiac couplet.

Elegy is a Greek word, coming from *legein*, to say, and *e*, meaning the noise you might make when powerful feelings overflow. Its purpose is the personal, the outpouring of one's own feelings, rather than the stately music of epic, with its space for narrative rumbling, and episodes tumbling from line to line. The elegiac couplet has one line that is as long as the epic line – six feet – and one that is shorter, and divided firmly into two pairs. The effect is to give an ineluctable cadence to each sentiment. Here it is at its most powerful:

> Traveler, take this word to the men of
> Lakedaimon:
> We who lie buried here did what they told us to do.[26]

Until his poems of exile, Ovid is seldom concerned to be so poignant. He even mocks the form in which he feels compelled to write, and at the start of his *Amores* blames Cupid for making the second line longer than the first (by laughing and stealing a foot). Here is the effect when Rolfe Humphries reproduces the rhythm in English:

> While you are footloose and free to play the field
> at your pleasure,
> Watch for the one you can tell, 'I want no other
> but you!'
> She is not going to come to you floating down
> from the heavens:
> For the right kind of a girl you must keep using
> your eyes.[27]

We should bear in mind that Ovid is writing Latin poetry in a metre invented for Greek; that Latin has a much smaller vocabulary than Greek; and that if you are going to write in this metre, half the words Latin has won't fit. This makes Ovid's achievement all the more astonishing. He writes about the day-to-day more than any other elegist: he includes the rules for board games, and even the formulae for face-masks, in his inflexible rhythm. And it is inflexible: Ovid is the one poet of the genre who adheres to the rules at their strictest.

So how can he manage to say anything at all? He does it by allusion, by periphrasis, and by some short cuts of his own. He seldom passes up opportunities to flash his learning at us, and, since he's using a Greek metre, will name mythological characters by their Greek patronymics, so that the Roman reader would need to know the Greek name for that character's father if he or she is to know what's going on.

This in turn presents a challenge to the translator. What is the best way to communicate Ovid's balance and playfulness in English? In introducing his own translation, Peter Green is clear:

Ovid has suffered, more than most Roman poets, from over-close association with the eighteenth century – an association which automatically guaranteed his depreciation during the Romantic revival . . . This relationship was given formal expression by the habit of translating his work into stopped rhyming couplets – a practice which obstinately survived even such hazards as the Ovidian habit of joking about Elegy's 'one lame foot' . . . the traditional translator, presumably unable to count, with cheerful impartiality gives him five on both.[28]

That is exactly what I've gone and done. I want to offer a brief defence. The English rhyming couplet, with its five feet in every line, has a lot in common with Ovid's metre. They *are* both stopped at the end of each pair of lines. If Ovid *were* around in the eighteenth century (and you can see him liking it), then his joke about Cupid could easily have been one about Milton. He could have been preparing to write an epic – *Paradise Lost*, say – and then found that Cupid had saddled him with an intrusive rhyme – the 'jingling sound of like endings' would provide Ovid with 'the troublesome and modern bondage of rhyming', and an equivalent to the bondage to which Cupid subjects his poets.

And anyway, there is a need to reflect Ovid's dexterity with a tight form. This isn't to say that any English translators have come at all close to his facility, although some first-rate versions have been made, from Dryden in the seventeenth century to Len Krisak in the twentieth.[29] The opportunity to translate Ovid is an invitation to a game, and just as Ovid's Latin, with its innuendoes, conceits and switches in tone, tricks us at every turn, so an English response should have fun.

Unlike Fielding, I have not attempted to update the poem. Not much, anyway. Early on I tried translating *vittae*, the woollen fillets worn by matrons, as Alice bands, as if these were an equivalent mark of modesty, but I abandoned this and tried to resist references to the modern world. (A reference to Beaujolais survives.) At times it has suited me to be literal; on other occasions, a small excursion from the Latin has brought the English closer to Ovid's directness. Like Peter Green, I have often gone for the 'silent gloss' – a rendering that sometimes explains an allusion as the English goes along. Some will find this an over-simplification, but some experience of discussing Ovid's poems in class tells me that even knowledgeable students will find the level of allusion sophisticated enough to understand how Roman readers would have felt sometimes smart and sometimes outsmarted.

My rule of thumb has been: if Ovid stumbled upon this translation, perhaps arriving in disguise to a Latin Composition Paper at university, and attempting the Verse option, would he be able to put it back into the Latin he hit upon in the first place? Well, yes, because he is the greatest, and if anyone could make something of this, it would be he. But if the below were capable of giving him a flicker, or even a smirk, of recognition, I should be satisfied.

I have used the Oxford Classical Text prepared by E. J. Kenney; from time to time I have adopted the readings of alternative manuscripts, or else of transpositions suggested by other editors, particularly Goold, Gibson and Hollis. I have referred to some moments of equivocation in the Notes.

ACKNOWLEDGEMENTS

I am hugely indebted to Amy Jenkins and Jonny Heawood for allowing me to spend a crucial week in their silent cottage. Bernard Holiday's suggestions for improvements were almost all unarguable. At Vintage, Liz Foley took on the project and gave excellent advice from the start; Frances Macmillan has seen it through with amazing patience and care. My agent, Karolina Sutton, has made the task easier. I don't know if the late Kate Jones appreciated how happy she made me when she arranged for me to do this. Her approval is as important to me as Ovid's.

None of this would have been possible without Louise, who has shown a kindness beyond reason, and tolerance beyond measure. Ovid knows that love is too important to be clear about. As his finest translator, Christopher Marlowe, puts it, 'Judge you the rest.'

Sherborne, October 2010

NOTES

1   *Amores* 3.7; 2.13 and 2.14

2   See *Tristia*, Letter 2.

3   *Ars Amatoria Selections* (Macmillan).

4   This argument is fair on the face of it, but it ignores something I find unavoidable: that the book for women is (even) better than the previous two. Some have found that Ovid is less psychologically acute in his treatment of women, and it is true that the Latin can be impersonal – he's more likely to say 'Let her . . .' than to issue a direct imperative. And yet his research into makeup is scholarly, his ordinances are self-denying, and the book is much more tightly organised: he wastes less time. For the purposes of his last book, he has learnt how to do a lot of things at once.

5   Fielding had already told her story in *The Female Husband: or, The Surprising History of Mrs Mary, alias Mr George Hamilton* (1746).

6   See 1.1 and 1.15, for example.

7   *Don Juan*, 3.8.

8   *The Art of Love* (hereafter *Art*) 1.501–2

9   *Art* 1.31–2

10 *Art* 1.585–6

11 *Art* 2.597–600: these lines are so strongly against adultery that they are sometimes considered spurious, but see note ad loc.

12 *Art* 3.57–8

13 *Art* 3.483–4

14 Ovid doesn't rule out sex with all slaves, though – the maid is available (as at *Amores* 2.7).

15 See discussion in Gibbon, 28ff.

16 *Dress and the Roman Woman: Self-Presentation and Society* (Routledge, 2008), p.27.

17 See note on *Art* 3.422

18 *Art* 3.33

19 *Amores* 1.8.

[20] *Tristia* 2.103

[21] Seneca, *Controversiae* 2.2, cited in Peter Green's introduction to his translation of Ovid, *The Erotic Poems* (Penguin, 1982).

[22] *Art* 2.359–72

[23] *Art* 3.301–6

[24] *Art* 2.501

[25] *Ovid Recalled*, p.310

[26] Simonides of Ceos, mourning the 300 Spartan dead at Thermopylae, translated by Richmond Lattimore.

[27] *Art of Love* translated by Rolfe Humphries (Indiana, 1957) quoted in *Rome: the Augustan Age*, edited by Kitty Chisholm and John Ferguson (Oxford, 1981).

[28] *The Erotic Poems*, p.78.

[29] This translation appeared in instalments in *PN Review*, and is awaiting publication from Carcanet. Dryden was joined by Congreve in his translation; the less brilliant Nahum Tate took on the *Cures*.

SELECT BIBLIOGRAPHY

Editions:

E. J. Kenney, *Amores, Medicamina Faceiei Femineae, Ars Amatoria, Remedia Amoris,* Oxford 1961

J. H. Mozley, *Ovid: The Art of Love and Other Poems* (Loeb), 1939, revised by G. P. Goold, 1979

Commentaries:

A. S. Hollis, *Ovid: Ars Amatoria Book I,* Oxford 1974

M. J. Griggs, *Ars Amatoria: Selections, ed. with an Introduction, Notes, Appendices and Vocabulary,* Macmillan, 1971

R. K. Gibson, *Ovid: Ars Amatoria Book 3,* Cambridge 2003

Translations:

P. Green, *Ovid: The Erotic Poems,* Penguin 1982

To Louise

elige cui dicas 'tu mihi sola places'

THE ART OF LOVE

BOOK 1

1   If you don't know the art of love, read on:
after this poem, you should be a don.
Oars make boats quick, but then, so does technique,
which speeds the chariot, and makes Cupid meek.
5   Automedon was skilled with reins and wheels;
Tiphys was master of the Argo's sails:
Venus made me an artist, worthy of
those legendary heroes, but for love.

Cupid's a rude boy, ready to attack,
10   but immature, and easy to push back.
Achilles had an old teacher, called Chiron,
who gave the boy a lyre to vent his ire on.
There's nobody Achilles can't deter,
and yet he's frightened of a pensioner,
15   and Hector benefited from each flog
felt from the hands of his harsh pedagogue.
They're legendary pros; I'm Cupid's teacher:
Cupid's a boy as much as heavenly creature.
Just as a plough weighs on a stout bull's neck,
20   and bits keep hardy-hearted steeds in check,
so Cupid yields to me, although he lands
darts in my chest, and harries me with brands.
Where Cupid hits, or burns with fiercer ardour,
my wounds will make me seek revenge still harder.

25 I don't acquire my skills from you, Apollo,[1]
    nor prophesy from some low-flying swallow;
    the nine Muses never appear to me
    when I compose didactic poetry.
    Experience prompts this. I'm a poet with art,
30 singing the truth. Venus, be at the start.

    No matron's bands. No signs of modesty.
    No skirts with hems much lower than the knee.
    Discreet seduction – safe sex – is my song,
    and in it, nothing is considered wrong.

35 1: Work to find out what you'd like to enamour;
    come at it as a soldier in new armour.
    2: Win over the woman you've impressed;
    3: Make sure that it's a love that time can test.[2]

    This is the course my chariot will cover –
40 the ground my wheel's permitted to go over.
    While you can go wherever (your lead's off),
    pick someone you can tell, 'Just you I love.'
    She won't come falling through the gentle skies;
    the right girl should be looked for with your eyes.
45 The huntsman knows this, stretching nets for stags –
    knows in what vale the gnashing wild boar lags –
    birdcatchers know their shrubs; hook-danglers
        know
    the waters where the biggest fish schools flow.

You also, scouting for a long affair:
50 the woman hangs out somewhere. Find out where.
I won't suggest the seeker should set sail –
you'll find your travel's not such a travail.
Sure, there's Andromeda, whom Perseus carries
from India, and the Greek girl fetched by Paris.
55 But Rome has so much talent you'll declare,
'Whatever the world has, you'll find it here.'
Like Gargara's crops, grapes on Methymna's vine,
and all species that trees and seas combine,
as numerous as the stars are girls in Rome,
60 Aeneas' town, where his mother's at home.

You want one fresh, still ripening in years?
Before your eyes, the very girl appears.
You settle on some bright young thing until
at Rome you find a thousand belles can thrill.
65 If you'd like one of later, wiser station,
trust me, they come in military formation.

Heat hits the Herculean lion's back – seek shade
and comfort under Pompey's colonnade,
or where, with marble cladding of great cost[3]
70 Octavia's gifts honour the son she's lost.[4]
And don't avoid Livia's portico,
scattered with its creator's new tableaux,
or where Danaids put their cousins to death,
and their hard father's sword's out of its sheath.[5]
75 Don't miss Adonis' shrine, where Venus weeps,

or Sabbath rites the Jew from Syria keeps,[6]
nor shrines to Io, heifer with golden curls
(who was for Jove what she's made other girls).[7]

Who would have thought law courts were good for
    love?
80   The spark's there, even in a lawyer's proof.
Yes, hard by Venus' temple, Appias wets
the air by pulsing water out in jets;[8]
that's where your counsel takes his brief from
    Cupid –
so smart with others' pleas, for his, he's stupid.
85   He who has left his statutes on the shelf,
in this deserted spot, pleads for himself.
The suitor is no longer pressing suits
and, stuck inside her temple, Venus hoots.

Best of all, love the theatre in the round;
90   you pray for love? Then this is fertile ground.
Whether you want to love, or just to play,
you'll find a one-night stand, or one who'll stay.
In long queues, ants go and come back again
conveying their provisions grain by grain,
95   and fragrances of thyme and nectar lead
bees buzzing flower by flower through the mead . . .
the most refined girls, likewise, rush to sports,
where many of them have detained my thoughts.
They come to look, and to be looked upon –
100   in this place, chastity and shame are gone.

Romulus first made games contentious, when
raped Sabine women sated single men.
Back then, no theatre veils hung from on high;
the stages weren't orange with saffron dye.
105   What branches grew in glady Palatine
were strewn to make the artless set design;
spectators sat on steps cut out of turf;
their hair was stuffed with twigs and thick with
     scurf.
They look, and register whom they like best,
110   and many things move in a silent chest;
And while the Pantomimist bangs his foot
thrice to the crude modes of a Tuscan flute,
during the claps (they clapped through joy, not
     duty),
the king signed to the crowd – Go get your booty.

115   Then up they sprang; expressed their minds with
     roars
and pounced upon the maids with lusty paws;
the frighted throng, as doves flee eagles, or
the lambkin flees the first wolf that it saw,
fled horrified by men rushing deranged –
120   whatever blush they had before was changed.
There was one dread, but not one face of dread:
some sat mindless; some tore hair from their head;
one begged, one was aghast, one stayed, another
ran, one went silent, one cried for her mother.
125   They were plunder, or trophies to collect:

their fear bestowed upon them some respect.
If some said no, or protested too much
men drew their quarry with a grasping clutch[9]
and said, 'Don't blur your tender eyes with dew;
130   what daddies are to mums, I'll be to you.'
Romulus knew what soldiers want for pay.
If I could earn that, I'd enlist today.
It's from this hallowed precedent, perhaps,
that modern theatres are such honey traps.

135   And don't rule out watching a chariot race –
the circus offers everyone a space.
Fingers that say things can't be intercepted;
a nod, too, can be noted and accepted.
If there's a vacant seat, sit by her side,
140   then put your side beside her side, and slide.
Don't worry if the rows create a squash –
house rules compel you and the girl to touch.
Your job is to strike up a friendly chat,
and platitudes can move from this to that:
145   eagerly ask about whose horse is whose;
the one she chooses is the one you'll choose.

When the parade of gods comes past your stand,
be sure to give Venus the warmest hand.
If dust falls in the girl's lap, don't delay –
150   this is your chance to finger it away.
Contingencies suit you – do what you must:
if there's no dust, finger away no dust,

and, if her clothes have lost too much of it,
be diligent; scoop up and spill some grit.
155 Obliging women thank you with this prize:
you get to keep a watch over her thighs.
And check the seat behind you, too, for fear
that someone's pressed his knee against her rear.
The little things ensnare light minds. It's grand
160 to plump her cushion with an easy hand.
Fanning the heavy air is always cool,
and propping up her sweet feet with a stool.

The place has many openings for a fling;
so does the sorry gladiator's ring.
165 Cupid has often wrestled in that dirt.
Those watching battles can themselves be hurt:
they talk, touch hands, they get the programmes in,
ask if the one they bet upon will win –
they've sensed the tender dart, groaned at the blow,
170 and have themselves become part of the show.

What of mock naval battles? Did you miss
our Caesar re-enacting Salamis?
From shore to shore, women and men left home
until the whole world snuggled into Rome.
175 Who couldn't find a lover in that throng?
How many felt the love that can't belong![10]

Caesar prepares to make our planet whole
by putting the Orient under his control.[11]

9

So, Crassus' grave, rejoice! Parthians, you'll crack:
180   the standards that you took are coming back.
Vengeance is here! A general young in age –
a boy wages a war boys shouldn't wage.[12]
Stop worrying about when gods are born:
among Caesars, strength has an early dawn.
185   A heavenly genius hastens on its way,
and hates losses through cowardly delay:
Hercules rivalled Jove; with his bare hands
he throttled snakes when still in swaddling bands;
Bacchus, you were the boy who you still are
190   when, with your wand, you conquered India.
With father's fortune, in his time, you'll fight;
in his time, with his fortune, show your might.
Under his name, you must fight novice wars,
you prince of youths (next, prince of senators).
195   You have brothers – avenge the brothers' sores;[13]
you have a father, so protect his laws.
Rome's father – yours – gives you warlike attire –
the foe takes kingdoms from your angry sire.
His darts are warped; your javelins are true:
200   Justice and Truth will be standards for you.
Parthians lose to our weapons, and our cause:
Caesar brings eastern riches to our shores.
Mars, Caesar, give the expedition force
(one is a god; one will be in due course).
205   I can smell victory, and shall rehearse
at my magniloquent best, my noblest verse:
recite it to your troops to give them grit

(oh may my lines be worthy of your spirit!).
I'll sing of Parthian backs, and Roman hearts,
210   of the enemy charging off, still firing darts.
Parthians, your tactic is the mock retreat –
how bad will that look when you're really beat!

Triumph will follow; you'll be golden when
white horses lead you, loveliest of men.
215   Ahead go conquered leaders, whose necks bow
beneath their chains – no flight for safety now.
The audience will be sat girl-boy, girl-boy;
on that day, every heart will burst with joy . . .

When a girl asks what king's being led away,
220   and what mountain or river's on display,
then answer everything – not just the questions
you can answer. Don't know? Then make
    suggestions:
this bloke's Euphrates – reeds are on his brow –
Tigris drips blue hair, like the water's flow;
225   look, some Armenians. Danae stands for Persia –
that Achaemenid valley town: don't perjure
yourself if you know this leader from that,
but just in case you don't, say something pat.

For starters, dining out is always fine,
230   where you'll be seeking something more than wine.
There, often, Love, with glowing purple face,
has steered the horns of Bacchus to their place,

and Wine's bespattered Cupid's spongy wing –
in captured ground, the boy is lingering.
235   But feathers flap – a sprinkle is enough
to intoxicate the affected breast with Love.
Wine primes the spirit – makes it apt with heat –
care vanishes when mixed with something neat.
Mirth follows; meek men raise their horny crowns[14]
240   and careworn foreheads lose dolours and frowns;
minds open; for the wine god can assuage
all the sophistication of our age.
Girls seize the souls of young men with desire:
Venus in vines is fire within a fire.
245   When lights are low, avoid judgement in haste:
darkness and drink severely harm your taste.
Paris saw goddesses on a clear day
when he said, 'Venus, take the prize away.'
Night pardons blemishes; it can conceal
250   all flaws, and everyone has sex appeal.
Examine precious jewels, purple dyes,
faces and bodies under open skies.[15]

There are so many hunting grounds, I'd rather
count sand than count places where women gather.
255   Of Baiae's beaches, north of Naples' bay,
and its hot, sulphurous springs, what can I say?
You'll moan: 'You said the water here was pure.
I've come back sicker than I was before.'
Suburbia holds Diana's glady shrine,
260   run by a priest slain by the next in line;

virgin Diana curses Cupid's darts;
yet she broke many, will break still more, hearts.[16]
So far we've had a sidelong glance at where
to lay traps – where to look for an affair.
265 What of the subtle skills you'll need to woo?
To explain, this poem must be subtle too.
Join me, and take my teaching with assurance,
and concentrate, men, even if you're morons.

First off, believe there's no one you can't get.
270 You'll capture someone: simply lay the net.
A hound would sooner scarper from a bunny
or grasshoppers stop singing when it's sunny
than any girl would pass up your advance –
even proposals you don't think she wants.
275 Discreet sex pleases woman, just as man;
she merely hides it better than he can.
It's better that the man express his need
than that a smitten woman take the lead.
The cow lows for her bull over the cud;
280 the mare neighs for her horny-footed stud.
In us, thank God, the raging lust's more tame,
and there's a limit to the manly flame.
Remember Byblis?[17] She longed to seduce
her brother; her urge ended in a noose.
285 To daddy, Myrrha's heart belonged too much,
so now she hides within the barky clutch
of trees diffusing fragrant tears of myrrh
(the oil that we import's named after her).[18]

Now, once there was a bull, pride of the males
290 that stomped around Mount Ida's shady vales
who was distinguished by a single blight –
a spot between his horns – the rest was white;
and every heifer miles around Mount Ida
would choose this bull of any bull to ride her.
295 But human Pasiphae rejoiced to be
his love, and eyed milkers with jealousy.[19]
Everyone knows: the hundred towns of Crete
admit it, famed as they are for deceit.[20]
Apparently, with dainty hands, she'd pull up
300 fresh leaves and meadow grass to feed her bull up.
The herd's friend has insouciance that mocks
her husband: Midas loses to an ox.
But Pasiphae, why dress up with such pride?
Wealth's meaningless to your bull-on-the-side.
305 Why use a mirror? You hang out with herds –
isn't your coiffure strictly for the birds?
At least your mirror says you're not a cow,
however much you crave horns on your brow!
Avoid affairs at all if you want happy ends,
310 but if you must, at least take *homo sapiens*.
She ran to woods and glades when Bacchus led
her like a Maenad from the marriage bed.
So often she would see a cow and gripe,
'I can't work out how she's my lover's type.
315 Get her, strutting about him in the grass.
She thinks she's beautiful; she's such an arse.'
She gave commands to chief bull: when she spoke

some harmless cow was put under the yoke
or led to where a botched-up altar stands –
320 she'd hold her rival's innards in her hands.
She'd please the gods with this intensive cull
and, grasping guts, cry out, 'Pleasure my bull!'
She wanted to be Io, or Europa
(one was a cow, and one a cow's eloper)
325 and tricked chief-bull, who tupped a cow of wood:
the progeny betrayed strange fatherhood.

Had Aerope laid off Thyestes' love
(abstaining from one man is hard enough!)
then never would the sun-god have turned back
330 to dawn, twisting his horses in mid-track.[21]
Scylla, whom love of Minos made purloin
her father's hair, now grinds hounds with her
        groin.[22]
One man faced war, sea-storms, surviving them –
        none
but his dreadful wife killed Agamemnon.
335 Creusa; murderous Medea; everyone's
wept through accounts of how she killed her sons.[23]
Through blinded eyes, wronged Phoenix's tears start
(Hippolytus' own steeds ripped him apart):
consider how your children's light is spent,
340 Phineus – that blinding is your punishment.

Everything feminine is ruled by lust:
it's more acute than ours, and more unjust.

So don't despair; all girls are worth a go,
and barely one of many will say no.

345　But yea or nay, the mere request can charm,
and if you don't succeed, then where's the harm?
Still, you'll not fail: when welcome pleasure swells,
isn't it better shared with someone else?[24]
Crops have more seed in someone else's field;

350　your neighbour's milkherd has a bigger yield.

First get to know the person who can aid
access to your intended girl: the maid.[25]
Make sure she's in on what her mistress thinks,
and seal the knowing deal with jokes and winks.

355　Corrupt her with enquiries and allures:
if she decrees it, what you seek is yours.
She has the girl's attention, and can choose
the moment (it's a technique doctors use);[26]
the mistress's attention's most secure

360　when she's content (crops flourish in manure).
When hearts are happy, unfettered from pain,
they are exposed, and Love's sailing is plain.
When Troy was sad, its walls were tight as coops;
when glad, in came the horse pregnant with troops.

365　When rivals pain her are the best of times;
then you can promise to avenge their crimes.
The maid, combing out bed hair, can endorse
the plan; she gives your sail the strength of oars,
and in a subtle murmur she can coo,

370　'You'd never treat that cheat as he treats you.'

Then talk's of you; her arguments conspire
with yours; she swears you'll die, mad with desire.
But hurry. Sails can droop; winds fade away:
like icicles, passion melts with delay.

375 'What if I do the maid?' I hear you cry.
If that's your game of dice, the stakes are high.
Sex that speeds one maid slows another down:
one renders you her boss's, one her own.
This is all chance. Fortune favours the brave,

380 but my advice will always be, behave.[27]
Young men shouldn't be caught, and won't be, if
I guide them, and we stay clear of the cliff.
But if she's taking messages for you
not just with zeal, but with her body too,

385 affairs don't start with maids, so if you stray,
boss takes priority; then the PA.
One warning, if my skills are to be trusted –
lest lessons went where greedy tempests blustered –
either don't try, or else go all the way.

390 In crime, your partner won't give you away.
The limed bird's useless that you didn't get;
likewise if boars escape a soggy net.
Let wounded fish dangle, then peel the hook:
unless you're going to win, don't even look.

395 [If she's complicit, she never betrays
but tells you what your mistress does or says.][28]
Conceal it well: if you conceal your spy,
your girlfriend stays under your watchful eye.

Timing: whoever thought seasons belong
400   to soil-tillers or sailors? Well, they're wrong.[29]
Corn doesn't always grow in tricky plots,
nor is green water always right for yachts,
nor will sweet girls fall safely for your baits:
you'll have two outcomes on two different dates.
405   If her birthday's at hand, or All Fool's Day,
when Mars and Venus (March and April) play,[30]
or when the Circus boasts the treasure store
of kings (not statues, as there were before),[31]
hold off: the constellation of the kid
410   portends tempests when it's submerged and hid;
stop what you're doing. If you think you'll float,
you'll hardly hold the wreckage of your boat.
Try Allia day: Romans commemorate
their bitterest defeat upon that date;[32]
415   it's good, like Sabbath, when the Jews are stopping
to rest, because there's less business – less
       shopping.[33]
Your girlfriend's birthday is the least auspicious – [34]
a dark day, when you give her what she wishes.
However well you dodge her, she'll discover
420   a way to pickpocket an eager lover.
The salesman sees your boutique-hungry girl;
you sit there; he has bounty to unfurl.
She'll make you look; as connoisseur, you eye it;
she'll give you kisses; then she'll make you buy it.
425   She'll treasure it for years, she will avow;
she needs it now; it's best to buy it now.[35]

You don't have cash about you? That's all right –
write out a cheque! (Why did you learn to write?)
You know she'll want a cake when birthdays dawn?
430 You'll be amazed how often she's been born.
You know she'll feign a loss, and shed a tear
while claiming that a gem fell from her ear?
If you have things she wants, she'll ask to use
    them;
and don't expect a thank you as you lose them.
435 To list each meretricious girl's technique
is more than ten mouths and ten tongues can
    speak.[36]

Send tablets (cleaned!)[37] of wax – see what they
    find –
wax can convey the firstlings of your mind.
It carries flattery and makes you sound
440 like lovers do; and let the praise abound.
Achilles gave back Hector after praise;[38]
when asked, an angry god can change his ways.
Make promises: they cannot harm your health.
With promises, you hint at boundless wealth.
445 Once she's believed, Hope holds for quite a while –
good goddess, Hope, because she can beguile.
But give your girl a gift, and off she'll trot –
she will have gained things past, while losing squat.
But if you don't give, seem about to give –
450 that's how a barren acre can deceive.
Gamblers who don't lose always make a loss –

dice whet the hungry hand for one more toss.[39]
Get with her giftless – that's the difficulty:[40]
she'll give out more, fearing she gave for free.[41]

455 So, send the letter, rich in compliment,
to travel and discover her intent:
Cydippe had to act on what she'd vowed –
ensnared because she read the words aloud.[42]
Learn proper skills, please, Romulus' descendants –

460 not only to protect timid defendants:[43]
like Senate, People and Judiciary,
girls give their hands, captured by oratory.
Still, hide the effect, and let your speech be far gone
from erudition or pretentious jargon.

465 What moron gives a sweetheart declamation?
Strong language often leads to consternation.
Keep speech convincing, words familiar,
and flattering, as if you spoke to her.[44]

If she won't read your note, and sends it back,

470 keep hoping that she'll read it – stay on track.
In time, bulls come to ploughs, and they submit;
horses, in time, bear the restraining bit.
An iron ring grows loose with much hard wear;
with hard-baked soil, in goes the plough's curved share.

475 Rock's hard, and water's soft, or so it seems
until hard rock's eroded by soft streams.
With time, you'll tame Penelope as well –[45]
Troy took a while to fall, and yet it fell.
She read, but won't reply? Then don't be pushy –

480 send her more things to read, and make them slushy.
If she enjoys the read, then she'll reply –
these things move by degrees from Low to High.
It's possible that her first notes demur
and ask you if you'll please stop bothering her.
485 She fears that; what she wants, she doesn't say;
so carry on – your godsend's on its way.

Meanwhile, if she's being carried down the street
upon a litter, make the approach discreet:
in case somebody's listening like a hawk,
490 add *double entendre* to your clever talk.
If she's scuffing along the colonnade
with idle feet, then join her promenade.
Precede her sometimes, and sometimes drop back;
speed up the pace, then let the pace go slack.
495 Don't be embarrassed if you want to slide
between pillars, or stand, side by her side;
if she goes to the theatre, you must go,
and from her shoulders upwards is your show.
Look at her: there's no law to stop you gawking,
500 so let eyebrows and gestures do the talking;[46]
applaud the mime who plays the woman's part –[47]
favour the third party who wins her heart.[48]
Rise when she rises; while she sits, sit still.
Waste time according to your girlfriend's will.

505 Don't wrench your hair around with iron pegs –
no pumice to defoliate your legs.

Those rites are for the eunuchs of Cybele
who ululate their Phrygian ditties gaily.[49]
Shabby chic works:[50] when Theseus bagged his girl
510   he didn't have a hairpin for his curl.
Phaedra desired Hippolytus ungroomed;
Adonis dressed for woods when Venus loomed.[51]
Be earthy, bronzed with martial exercise;[52]
make sure your toga's spotless, cut to size.
515   Don't have a rigid tongue, or rusty teeth;[53]
no foot should be at sea in some slack sheath.
Don't let a dodgy cut deform your hair;
both your coiffure and beard need trusted care.[54]
Avoid protruding nails blackened with mire;
520   your nostrils should be clear of any wire.
Don't let the halitosis from your throat
irk any noses like a billy goat.[55]
Anything more's for slappers, or perhaps
the sort of chap who's after other chaps.[56]

525   Look! Bacchus calls his poet: he's aflame
and comes to help lovers who feel the same.[57]
The Cnossan Ariadne woke to find
herself on strange Naxos, out of her mind;
and, as from sleep, she left her dressing gown
530   undone. Barefoot, her blonde hair tumbling down,
she cursed cruel Theseus; but no wave would hear;
her cheek softened with an indignant tear.
She cursed and cried at once – both were in keeping –
she was no less attractive for her weeping.

535 She said, pounding her chest over and over,
     'What is my fate? He's left, my lying lover.
     What is my fate?' With cymbals, all the strand
     resounded, and with drum, and pulsing hand.
     She fell in fear, with no more to exclaim
540 as all the blood drained from her lifeless frame.
     Look! Satyrs! Bacchants – see their hairy backs;
     their god will follow shortly in their tracks.
     Silenus, look, is drunk; his posture's wonky;
     He holds (somehow) the thick hair on his donkey.⁵⁸
545 Bacchants seek him and flee him; he plays tag,
     poor knight, plying a rod to goad his nag,
     slips from his long-eared steed, and bangs his brain,
     while satyrs yell, 'Rise, father, rise again!'
     Now god! He'd decked his chariot with grape –
550 it's hitched to tigers – gold reins in his grip;
     the girl had lost her man, her voice, her blush;
     thrice she sought flight; thrice fear held back her
         rush.
     She bristled like a stalk when winds are harsh,
     or like a lily in a ruffled marsh.
555 Bacchus told her, 'I'm loyal, at your side –
     the girl from Cnossos will be Bacchus' bride.
     The sky's your dowry; there's your constellation –
     the Cretan crown helps boats with navigation.'⁵⁹
     He jumped down from his chariot, lest she dread
560 his tigers, moved sand with his godlike tread,
     and, as she didn't fight him, he could seize
     her to his breast – gods do all that with ease.⁶⁰

'Hymen!' some sing, and others roar, 'Evoe!'[61]
The couple's on the couch, and off they go.
565 Dinners are circumstances that combine
a couch, a girl, you and the god of wine,
so pray to him, that creature of the night,
in case the drinking puts your brain to flight.[62]
Share secrets cryptically, and converse
570 in language that she'll feel's uniquely hers:[63]
write on a tabletop in subtle wine
and let your mistress read your chat-up line;
let speaking eyes show passion, each to each:
often a silent face has words, and speech.
575 Make sure you grasp the cup first, which her lip
has touched, and where she sipped, that's where
you sip;
when she fingers the food, finger it, and
let your hand linger till it feels her hand.
Charming her boyfriend is a worthy end –
580 he'll be more useful to you as a friend.[64]
You've won a drink? Then let him drink instead;
give him the crown that's fallen from your head.
He's after you, or level? Yield your place;
strongly agree with everything he says.
585 It's safe and customary to cheat on friends;
customary, but a criminal offence.
Managers over-manage: they believe
they should poke into things beyond their brief.[65]
Don't drink more units than the accepted norm:[66]
590 your brain and feet have duties to perform.[67]

Beware of arguments goaded by drink,
and hands that go too swiftly to the brink.
His reckless drinking killed Eurytion,[68]
so food and wine are better kept for fun.

595 If you can sing, sing; if you're lithe-limbed, dance –
charm by whatever gift gives you the chance.[69]
Real drunkenness offends; false drunks delight –
those slippery souls that can't say 's's right:[70]
you show yourself more shameless than you
    should,

600 and everyone will reckon that you're stewed.
Then toast the dame, and toast the man who's hers,
although your mind harbours a secret curse.

But when the company's going away,
you'll have access in the departing fray.

605 Insert yourself within the city's flow,
and touch – fingers to side, or toe to toe.
It's time for talking: banish rustic cares:
Venus and Fortune favour him who dares.
No need to be poetically correct –

610 say what you want, with native intellect.
Your role's the lover: mimic wounds with language;
by any trick, persuade her of your anguish.
Persuasion's easy – all girls think they're fit –
even the plainest is convinced of it –

615 but often, actors feel the things they show:
often, what he pretends is so, is so.[71]
(Women, be kind to people who pretend:

false love now could be true love in the end.)
Now seize on her slyly – flannel to court her:
620   by river banks there lurks the clear, calm water.[72]
Don't tire of praising face and hair; her sweet
fingers, so well proportioned! Such small feet!
And virgins, too, are thrilled by eulogies –
virgins are keen to know their faces please.
625   Poor Juno and Minerva: how it taints them
that Paris' decision went against them.
Juno's peacock fans feathers if you praise them:
if you stay silent, then he'll never raise them.[73]
Competitive racehorses love the reins
630   if you've patted their necks and groomed their
        manes.

Promises win women. Don't be afraid
to summon any deity to your aid.[74]
Jupiter's always laughed when lovers lied
and bids the breeze take oaths ungratified.
635   He'd swear to Juno by the River Styx,
perjuring. He can teach us all some tricks.
We worship gods out of expedience:[75]
old households gave them wine and frankincense.
No cosy rest for them:[76] nothing like sleep:
640   live blamelessly, because their power is deep.
Give back deposits; piously keep faith;
avoid all fraud and keep hands free of death.
If bending rules, bend them for girls alone –
in these affairs, faith's harder to condone.

645 So cheat, so cheat on them. It's only fair:
most are profane; catch them in their own snare.
It's said that once, Egypt had gone without
refreshing rain, and felt nine years of drought,
when Thrasias told Busiris, 'Please the God
650 and get a foreigner to spill his blood.'
Busiris then replied, 'You'll be the first –
the foreigner whose gift will quench our thirst.'[77]
Perillus, too: cruel Phalaris[78] tormented
him in the very bull-kiln he'd invented.
655 And neither king made a decision wiser
than turning a device on its deviser.
It's only justice, then, to lie to liars:
let woman feel the outrage she inspires.[79]

Tears work; for crying, adamant gives way;
660 if possible, put damp cheeks on display.
Still, tears don't always happen on demand;
if not, then wipe your hand with moistened hand.
To mix kisses with flattery is wise –
if she won't give, then take what she denies.
665 She'll fight at first, call you a ghastly chap;
she wants, though, to be conquered by a scrap.[80]
Only, ensure that snatched kisses don't scuff
her tender lips; she'll say you were too rough.
A man who takes the kisses, and no more
670 doesn't deserve the things she gave before.
How close was he to something still more pleasant?
It's not because he's modest, but a peasant.

Force is allowed:[81] girls like a certain sort:
they're often less reluctant than they thought.

675 The trespassing amour that's won by theft
delights; the wickedness is like a gift.
Drivable girls, if they retire unhad,
might well look happy, but they're really sad.
Phoebe felt force; her sister, too, was seized;

680 the plunderer and the plunder both were pleased.[82]

It's worth telling a tale, often relayed,
that links Achilles to a Scyrian maid.
In Ida's vale, Venus, who fairly won
a beauty prize, gave treasure of her own –

685 the daughter-in-law that King Priam let come –
the Greek girl, in the walls of Ilium.
Everyone swore to heal her husband's sores,[83]
and one man's pain became a people's cause.
Shamefully – he was under duress –

690 his mother begged – Achilles wore a dress.
What were you doing? Weaving's not your game:
Athene's other gift will win your fame.[84]
What's with the baskets? Get your shield, and
    train –
your Hector-slaughtering hand's holding a skein.

695 Toss out that spindle, wrapped in tricky thread –
that hand should shake the Pelian spear instead.[85]
By chance, a royal virgin shared his chamber;
she proved he was a man, because he shamed her.
So she was won by strength, we must conclude,

28

700   and yet, by strength, she wanted to be wooed.
        'Come back!' she'd say, when he rushed off to don
        his manly arms, and cast off casting on.
        Deidamia, where's the force now, when you aim
        to keep Achilles, author of your shame?
705   The blame's on the initiator's part –
        your pleasure's in letting the other start.
        A young man has excessive confidence
        in how he looks if he lets girls commence.
        The man begins; the man has to beseech;
710   the girl's job's to accept his pretty speech.
        Get going – make your motion manifest:
        she begs the question. You require. Request.
        Jupiter begged the ancient heroines –
        girls don't corrupt Jupiter with their sins.
715   But if your praises pamper her conceit,
        attack less – make a tactical retreat.
        Most girls reject what's here, and love what goes;
        eliminate boredom: don't stand so close.
        Asking won't always serve your amorous ends –
720   love lurks under the cover of being friends.
        I've seen some stubborn girls won by this plan –
        who was her handyman, is now her man.

        No one expects a sailor to be white –[86]
        when he's at sea, he's darkened by the light;
725   nor should the farmer, plying ploughs to move
        the earth beneath the blazing glare of Jove,
        and athletes, training for the Olympic crown

should be ashamed unless their skin is brown.
White suits the lover.[87] Every lover's pale.
730   It's common knowledge that the fair prevail.
Orion palely loitered for love's dream;
Daphnis went pale for his nymph of the stream.[88]
Leanness proves that you're serious, and it's good
to hide your goldy locks with the invalid's hood.[89]
735   Night vigils and the agonising rigour
of deep love whittle away a young man's figure.
If you're to gain your heart's desire, look rough,
so anyone can see that you're in love.

Need I complain we muddle good and bad?
740   Many who've trusted friendship have been had.
Don't brag of your beloved to a chum;
if he believes your praises, in he'll come.[90]
'Patroclus never shamed Achilles' bed –
Phaedra held off Pirithous,' some have said;
745   'Pylades and Hermione didn't sin –
like Castor and Helen, he loved her as a twin.'[91]
You hope the same? Then hope that honey slushes
midstream, and apples sprout from tamarisk
    bushes.[92]
Vice alone cheers; each craves his own relief –
750   gratification comes from others' grief.
Don't fear your enemies! Yes, it's unjust –
you're safer steering clear of those you trust.
Your boon companions, relatives and brothers –
this crowd is permanent among your bothers.

755 I'll finish soon. Girls have such differing hearts.
　　Thousands of minds require thousands of arts.
　　Not all soils suit all crops – some bear the vine,
　　others bear olives; in some, wheat is fine.
　　Hearts' ways diversify as looks in faces –
760 smart men adapt themselves to endless cases.
　　Like Proteus, they'll assume the lion's roar,
　　then be a tree, a wave, a hairy boar.[93]
　　Some fish need trawling; some go in the net,
　　some finish up on hooks when bait is set.
765 Trap different ages in a different style:
　　old does will spot your tactics from a mile.[94]
　　Seem wise to rough girls, pushy to the meek,
　　and it's not you, but misery they'll seek.
　　Such girls would sooner hug a bounder than
770 settle themselves down with an honest man.

　　Part of this work is fore, and part is aft.
　　Still, here let's weigh the anchor of my craft.

NOTES

1 Ovid achieves two things at once with this claim. One is that he follows the tradition of didactic, or informative poetry: he claims that he has special knowledge of the subject at hand, and that he is uniquely well-informed. In this, he follows Callimachus, the especially learned Greek poet (and librarian at Alexandria) whose *Aitia* (*Causes*) begin with a similar boast: 'I tell you to take a path which carriages do not wear down; don't take a chariot down other people's tracks, nor take a wide throughway, but on untrodden paths . . .' The other achievement is to remind the reader that love itself is an experience unique to the lover. The Latin love poet will naturally make a play of this, and argue that he is more worth reading because he feels love more acutely: cf. Propertius, 1.7:

> Then you'll reflect that I'm no rhyming hack –
> you'll rate me more than any Roman brain;
> youths mourning at my grave won't hold this back:
> 'Here lies Propertius, poet of my pain.'

2 This becomes the subject of Book 2.

3 Ambiguity: marble on the outside, or marble from outside (i.e. foreign)?

4 Augustus' sister Octavia was the mother of Marcellus, the great hope as successor to Augustus as Caesar. Book 6 of Virgil's *Aeneid* ends with a vision of the boy in the underworld.

5 Augustus' temple to Apollo was associated with the children of the brothers Danaus and Aegyptus. The fifty sons of Aegyptus followed the fifty daughters of Danaus from Egypt to Greece, and married them. On the wedding night, all but one of the daughters killed their new husbands. In Latin, the phallic connotations of swords were even more obvious than they are now.

6 Any rites were an opportunity to see women; curiosity would bring women to these festivals.

7 Io is often identified with Isis, the Egyptian goddess: if women fall in love at her temple, then she makes them as smitten as she was with Jupiter.

⁸ Appias was a water nymph. Hollis notes, 'a jet of water spurts out under high pressure, possibly from the mouth of the nymph'.

⁹ Literally, with a desirous lap; 'to a lusty crotch' is tempting.

¹⁰ Literally, a foreign love tortured so many. (Cf. Groove Armada's 'Why does it feel so good?')

¹¹ Gaius Caesar was Augustus' grandson, and designated heir. He was nineteen when he undertook this mission to Parthia. This is a propemptikon – a send-off – in which Ovid seeks to establish the support of Augustus. For Ovid to write this kind of thing, with this degree of enthusiasm, suggests the lines of Auden in 'The Truest Poetry Is The Most Feigning', in which a poet is advised to cross out his beloved's name and insert that of the latest dictator.

¹² Boy: an echo of Ovid's familiar term for Cupid (as, for example, l. 18)? The difficulty in translating this passage lies in gauging how reverent or irreverent Ovid is being. It is tempting to make him seem cheeky and over-familiar with the establishment. For example, 'Caesar', which sounds like a formal title to us, is simply a surname to the Roman ear (although admittedly a dynastic one).

¹³ A reference to brothers held hostage by the Parthian king.

¹⁴ The horns here symbolise animal strength, rather than cuckoldry.

¹⁵ Delia Smith gives advice from the other side of this equation, with economy and zeugma that Ovid would surely envy: 'And don't be tempted to skimp on the candles – they'll flatter the room, you and your food.' (*How to Cheat at Cooking*, 1971)

¹⁶ Diana's temple at Nemi is (among other things) the central image of James Frazer's *The Golden Bough*: its central mystery is what lies behind this and other rituals of killing and sacrifice? The book's epigraph is a snatch of Lord Macaulay's *Lays of Ancient Rome*: 'Those trees in whose dim shadow/The ghastly priest doth reign/The priest who slew the slayer,/And shall himself be slain.' In Ovid's lines, meanwhile, Diana can be seen to afflict people precisely because she is a goddess of chastity. She is also goddess of childbirth, and brings its attendant pains.

¹⁷ In case you didn't – she falls in love with her brother Caunus. Ovid talks more about this in *Metamorphoses*, Book 9.

18   This snippet of aetiology – glossing the roots of the word myrrh – might seem callously smartalec in this context, but throughout this passage, Ovid's showing off is stylised and conventional. He is merely proving that he falls into the category of learned poet (*doctus poeta*).

19   Pasiphae, wife of Midas, king of Crete, falls in love with a bull; she becomes the mother of the Minotaur.

20   Ovid is alluding to the paradox of the Cretan lies. The philosopher Epimenides was from Crete, and said, 'All Cretans lie.' So was this Cretan lying? And if Ovid is reworking the paradox, is *he* lying? If he is, then it could be for aesthetic reasons: to wrongfoot us with an irreverent question about the power of myth. But A. S. Hollis offers a more consistently classical way to suggest that Ovid's telling the truth: 'Ovid gives the proverb an unexpected twist: here is no false story which the Cretans have invented for their own advantage, but a true and discreditable one which they cannot deny!'

21   Ovid rounds off this section with an inventory of women whose unruly desires had tragic consequences: Aerope was married to Atreus, but fell in love with Atreus' brother, Thyestes. Atreus' revenge was to feed Thyestes his own sons. Atreus was the father of Agamemnon. This banquet was one of the factors that contributed to Agamemnon's death: Aegisthus, son of Thyestes, takes his own revenge on the house of Atreus in the blood feud. Another factor, though, is Clytemnestra, Agamemnon's wife, who is avenging Iphigenia, the daughter Agamemnon sacrificed so that favourable winds could blow the Greek ships to Troy. This isn't what she's doing in this passage, though: she is here because of her unlawful desire for Aegisthus. (In Aeschylus' play *Agamemnon*, Clytemnestra is portrayed as transgressively masculine, which fits the counter-intuitive account of femininity that Ovid is offering.) Phoenix is blinded for sex with his stepmother; Phineus is blinded for being a prophet who revealed the plans of Zeus. It is an odd fit here, but G. Devereux, cited by Hollis (ad loc.), has looked at blinding as a punishment for sexual crimes; Phineus' punishment involves his children's blindness: the sins of the father are visited upon the son, a line which Ibsen applies to congenital syphilis in *Ghosts*.

²² Ovid is conflating two myths here; or else, giving an unpleasant twist to one of them. The girl who betrayed her father is Scylla; Minos is besieging her town, and she gives him a lock of her father Nisus' hair, which leads to the town's downfall. Ovid combines this with another Scylla – the monster who, comprising of dogs, can snaffle six of Odysseus' men at a time.

²³ Medea killed her sons to punish her husband Jason when he left her for Creon's daughter Creusa.

²⁴ This line is literally: when things that are other/not yours (*aliena*) capture [your] mind with theirs. The stress on *aliena* is curious: is Ovid being as subtle as Auden in 'Alone', 'it must be shown/Why every lover has a wish to make/Some other kind of otherness his own . . .'? Or is the *aliena* set up in contrast to the sort of pleasure one can have oneself? If so, the analogy could be with the messenger in *Asterix in Switzerland* whose errand means he has to miss an orgy. He is given a packed orgy, which he later discards, saying, 'An orgy's no fun on your own.' The next couplet suggests that Ovid has another sin in mind: coveting something that belongs to somebody else.

²⁵ Ovid deals with this predicament in a riveting diptych. His *Amores* (2.7 and 2.8) show him fending off accusations from his girlfriend that he has been with the maid, Cypassis; and in the subsequent poem he asks Cypassis how the girlfriend could ever have learnt about the twist. The sequence ends with a devious blackmail – or at least, the suggestion that if the maid squeals, the result will be mutually assured destruction. (For more on corruption and bribery, see the routine about chaperones at *Art of Love* Book 3 (hereafter *Art*), especially ll. 651–2.) Here, Ovid's advice is still more pragmatic, and at Book 1, ll. 390 shows that the Cypassis episode is an application of theory.

²⁶ Cf. the moment in *Swann's Way* when Swann wants to ask Odette one more time if she has slept with women: 'However, he would not let her go but sat there like a surgeon waiting for a spasm to subside that has interrupted his operation but will not make him abandon it.' *Remembrance of Things Past*, Vol. 1, p. 394 (translated by Terence Kilmartin).

27 Hollis (ad loc.) quotes the convincing view of R. Pichon, writing in 1902: 'Ovid discusses these grey areas as a jurist might expound on a contested case of civil law.' Certainly the subject quickly brings out the equivicator in the poet.

28 These lines are unlikely to be by Ovid (Merkel's excision is widely accepted), and even if they are, they've fetched up at an odd moment in the argument. It reads like a verse précis of the passage, or else as filler copy in the perceived absence of some other line.

29 The style, scope and imagery of this link is a gesture towards didactic poetry, particularly Virgil's *Georgics*, with its attention to seasonal variations.

30 March is named after Mars; Venus was worshipped on 1 April (the Kalends) by women of all classes – matrons, freedwomen and prostitutes.

31 Ovid's joke here is that birthdays and market days are bad days for lovers, because you end up having to buy gifts for your beloved. For the Circus joke to work, it's helpful to imagine the venue as a vast Christmas market. Ovid's aside adds another level of satire: that in the old days, shoppers would be content with clay or pastry figurines. Unlike other, more moralistic poets, Ovid does not deplore these developments; at *Art* 3.101–34, and *Treatments for the Feminine Face* (hereafter *Treatments*) ll. 11ff., the elegist revels in the tastes of his sophisticated readership.

32 An intriguing dig at decency: Allia day – 18 July – commemorated the Romans' defeat at the hands of the Gauls in 390 BC. Ovid's posture of excitement is as tasteful as partying on Remembrance Sunday, only with national humiliation thrown in.

33 Griggs' school edition is fairly quick to make the link between Judaism and trade. But given the social mix of Rome at the time, this is unlikely to be such an easy conclusion. As Hollis remarks, 'it does not appear that Roman Jews engaged in commerce more than other occupations'. His note on *Art* 1.76 adds, 'The Jewish religion . . . probably helped to establish a seven-day week in Rome.'

34 Another reversal joke: birthdays were given all the attention that

we give them now: see Propertius 3.10, to which these lines read as an antidote.

[35] Griggs (p. 109) approves of this as an example of Ovid's timeless acuity. I was all set to disagree in the present note, but just as I was translating this, my wife was in an auction house in Dorchester, and came back with an urgent need to buy a stuffed zebra for the hallway.

[36] Actually, Ovid had a go at this. The premise of *Amores* 1.8 is that the poet overhears a *lena* – a brothel madame – instructing a prodigy on how to get the most out of a man (including the cake ruse). Ovid is even more bitter there than he is in the pay-off here (which is bitter enough given the tone of social comedy that precedes it). That poem is a vital one for understanding the whole tone of the *Art*. As Roy Gibson observes of *Art* 3, in which the poet advises women, the voice of the *lena* works as a counterpoint to the voice of the didactic poet in the line of Hesiod.

[37] The Roman reader would have understood this aside instantly; modern readers will have to wait until *Art* 2.396 and 3.495.

[38] A reference to Achilles restoring Hector's body to his father, Priam, for burial.

[39] 'Mark [Griffiths, Professor of Gambling Studies at Nottingham Trent University] puts forward this theory of a "near miss" with "hardened gamblers" not constantly losing but constantly nearly missing. On a cognitive level they (the gamblers) turn all these losing experiences into near wins.' (www.psychblog.co.uk/interview-the-gambling-man-prof-mark-griffiths-119.html; accessed 1 September, 2010).

[40] An echo of Virgil's *Aeneid*, 6.129: 'but to recall your steps, [from the underworld] to escape to the breezes above, this is your task, your work.' Ovid's allusion hints at the *adunaton* – the expression of an impossible idea. The satirical note becomes the innuendo that women almost never give for free.

[41] The 'give' pun lurks in Ovid's original: *ne dederit gratis quae dedit, usque dabit*. A comparison with a passage in *Art* 3.463–6 reveals a

traditional double standard: there, as at *Amores* 1.8, women are berated for accepting gifts and giving nothing in return, whereas here men are advised on how to achieve the same something-for-nothing. The lawyer Ovid, skilled in the *controversia*, can alternate between considering it gift exchange or prostitution depending on context and direction of argument. (Book 1, l. 658 offers a related justification for men to do things women do with impunity: it's tit-for-tat, and women started it.)

42 Acontius tricked Cydippe into marrying him by writing, 'I swear by Artemis that I will marry Acontius' on an apple. In ancient times, almost nobody read silently (Julius Caesar in the senate was an impressive exception), and the act of reading these words aloud made Cydippe feel that she was under oath.

43 The poet explores the issue of whether lawyers can be persuasive wooers. Cf. l. 83, above.

44 When advising women on how to write letters, Ovid offers similar advice (*Art* 3.479–82ff.): they are not to sound barbaric, nor too clever.

45 A passing attack on Augustus' high standards of morality? The most stable figures are fair game in the *Art*. Penelope appears again as a beacon of feminine probity at *Art* 3.15.

46 As this follows a prescriptive passage about language, it's worth noting how often so verbally playful a poet as Ovid turns his skill to situations in which people cannot, or do not speak: cf. on dinner parties (ll. 565–68), and in *Amores* 1.4. In Book 3 of his *Metamorphoses*, Ovid wrings the pathos out of Echo's inability to speak. In this case, conversation is difficult because men were no longer seated with women in the theatre.

47 As Hollis notes, women were allowed to take part in the mime, but just as often didn't.

48 A delicate piece of Zhdanov-dodging. Ovid isn't allowed to encourage adultery, which was punishable after 18 BC. But he does manage to do it indirectly, as if blaming characters in a play; and, when that play obeys the rudiments of old Roman comedy, he is showing how the stock love-triangle characters – the stupid husband,

the wily swordsman and the colluding wife – have always been part of mainstream Roman culture.

49 Ovid is quick to mock effeminacy in men. The cult of Cybele, the great mother goddess, was conspicuously eastern; a notable Roman exploration of it comes from Catullus (63), in which men take the part of her lover Attis, and castrate themselves.

50 Literally, a neglected beauty becomes a man.

51 A neat exploration of two corresponding myths, all the neater because Ovid isn't exploring the point at which they correspond. Aphrodite caused Hippolytus' death, which cost Artemis her dearest devotee; a line at the end of Euripides' *Hippolytus* suggests that the death of Adonis is Artemis' revenge. Here, though, the heroes are linked by their attitudes towards couture.

52 Similarly, Horace despairs of a young man called Sybaris, who is in love and no longer works out on the Campus Martius (*Odes* 1.12).

53 This line, as it appears in the manuscripts, has needed constant tweaking; the direction in which you tweak depends on whether you think the nouns refer to part of the mouth or part of the shoe. I've gone for the shoe. Hollis (a persuasive shoe man) quotes a line of Horace, about a scruff: 'His toga waved down rustically from his hair, and his badly loosened shoe stuck to his foot.' (Horace's Satires, 1.3.31-2)

54 It has been observed – by Cat Deeley and perhaps others – that a haircut is a more important investment than clothes, because the clothes you may wear only a few times, whereas you are constantly wearing your hair. (Cited by an unnamed participant in *Mary Queen of Shops*, Series 3, Episode 5.)

55 For practical advice on this complaint, see *Art* 3.277–8.

56 This avoidance of extremes will emerge as a hallmark of Ovid's style. The poet's line on homosexuality is a little jibing at times, but more characterised by an attitude of 'Thanks, but no thanks.' He develops the idea of the effeminate man at *Art* 3.447–8, when he tells women to avoid him (he'll start raiding your wardrobe). Sex between men was not in itself offensive to Romans, but the issue

of who was penetrating whom was a greater concern, and a matter of status. See *Art* 2.688 and note.

[57] Bacchus = Dionysus, god of wine, lord of misrule, the deity celebrated in the annual springtime festival of drama in Athens, etc. Titian's *Bacchus and Ariadne* is a faithful depiction of Ovid's vignettes on this theme (another occurs in his *Letters of the Heroines,* and in his *Fasti,* Book 3). Hollis calls this an 'attractive digression'. It's certainly attractive, but less like digressing than splicing.

[58] You can see this in the background of the Titian painting (National Gallery, London).

[59] Her crown turned into stars.

[60] A reminder, in the didactic tradition, that what he's advising to mortals is hard (cf. 2.233ff.).

[61] Hymenaeus is the mythical figure who leads wedding processions; the name provides the refrain in Catullus' epithalamium (61). He looked like a girl, and so accidentally accompanied some Athenian women who were captured by pirates as sacrificial offerings. He killed these pirates, and because he was then able to marry his noble-born beloved – whom he had stalked – he was remembered forever afterwards at marriage ceremonies. Evoe is one of the spontaneous shouts that provide extra names for Dionysus.

[62] At this point, it becomes likely that the whole *Ariadne auf Naxos* excursion was a ploy, both to up the mythological anecdote count, and to wheel the poem (back) around to one of Ovid's hobby-horses, the dinner party. The shamelessness of this construction is surely self-knowing, in the manner of Sterne.

[63] See note 46, above. *Amores* 1.4 is a try-out for this passage: there, the poet gives his (illicit) mistress commands in a way that anticipates the prescriptive tone here. This makes the comparison revealing: the persona of *Amores* can boss his lover around in the same way that a *preaceptor amoris* – a love don – can assert himself here. (Still, *Amores* 1.4 does have a forlorn cadence, suggesting that the man there has nothing like the control he wants.)

[64] Again, as at *Amores* 1.4, the woman's more open partner is present,

and is designated as 'vir' – man – rather than something more specific such as *maritus*; another sign of treading carefully in Augustus' Rome. For another constructive use of the fine line between love-rival and comrade, see *The Cures for Love* (hereafter *Cures*) 791–4.

65 Some editors have questioned these four lines, and Peter Green is confident that they are spurious, because they seem to spell out too crudely the 'Don't try this at home' message in a way that seems like a direct response to Augustus' laws on adultery. But I'd argue for keeping them: the second couplet has a double-edged piquancy that would be impressive in an interpolator. To make the cut under-estimates Ovid's versatility as a satirist, as capable of Swiftian sarcasm as he is of other modes.

66 In *Cures* 809, Ovid finds an argument in favour of drinking too much.

67 Feet? Yes – dancing, and getting home safely. Hollis, ad loc., cites a line of Terence as giving feet an official duty: 'When I got up neither my foot nor my brain was up to its task.' (*Eunuchus*, 729)

68 A centaur, killed in the fight with the Lapiths, at the wedding of Hippodamia (whom Eurytion tried to abduct on that difficult occasion).

69 Along with pleas for moderation, another refrain of Ovid's is that you should play to your own strengths. This shows a poet relaxed with the idea of individualism – an idea which, because it was less developed in ancient times than in ours, needed regular assertion. Cf. 755ff. and later on sexual positions that flatter one's particular figure (3.772).

70 At *Art* 3.294–5, women are told that there's a limit to how much they should affect lisps. And at *Art* 3.765–6, women are warned off excessive drinking.

71 This Clintonian method of self-persuasion turns out to be useful when recovering from love, too: *Cures* 489ff.

72 A line that makes more sense in the light of 1.475–6 above.

73 Ovid makes the peacock feminine, but it's hard to be comfortable

with this in the light of 'My Conviction' in *Hair*: 'There is a peculiar notion that elegant plumage / And fine feathers are not proper for the man / When actually that is the way things are in most species.'

74 The joke about Agamemnon at *Cures* 784 is a shade more respectful of the gods.

75 This widely quoted line has sometimes been taken as a sign of Ovid's impiety. This is a mistake: as the following lines suggest, they are expedient because they act as the kind of bogeymen who scare citizens into social cohesion. As ever, though, Ovid is warning against excessive restrictions on behaviour (for which the gods themselves could provide support: see, for examples, Euripides' *Hippolytus* and *The Bacchae*). It was perfectly possible to bandy these views about, even in the prevailing moral climate: these lines are more reverent than the much-read poetry of Lucretius, to which they seem to allude; and in any case, the unsuccessful attempts of Caesar to have himself deified (just before Ovid was born) remind us that affairs of the next world were, at the very least, negotiable for the residents of the present one.

76 Lucretius (c.94 BC – c.55 BC), following the Greek philosopher Epicurus, argues that gods do not influence events in this world (*On the Nature of Things*, e.g., at 1.62ff.).

77 For more on the links between blood and agriculture, see the chapters, 'Woman's Part in Primitive Agriculture' and 'The Corn-Mother and Corn-Maiden' in Sir James Frazer, *The Golden Bough*.

78 Phalaris was a tyrant of Acragas in Sicily (c. 6th century BC). The idea of a person being inside a fake cow has echoes of the Pasiphae story above.

79 See note 41 (on l.454) above.

80 This is consistent with other 'no means yes' expressions from Ovid (e.g., l. 126) above, and a sharp reminder of the risks we run if we assume his advice is applicable today. The earlier elegist Tibullus seeks to establish what sort of force is acceptable: beating is wrong, but ripping clothes or pulling hair is permissible. (Ovid points out later that this is unreliable, but 2.169–72 at least shows

that Tibullus was reaffirming what were then standard liberties and limitations.)

[81] Duncan Kennedy shows how this line is ambiguous in Latin: he translates it as 'You are permitted to apply force', while adding, 'The range of application of the Latin verb *appellare* permits another translation of line 673: 'though you may call it "force", that sort of "force" is pleasing to girls.' *The Arts of Love* (Cambridge, 1993), 55.

[82] Either Ovid is using this episode to suit himself, or is using a source that hasn't survived. Phoebe and her sister Hilaira were abducted by Castor and Pollux, when they were engaged to others.

[83] I.e. Menelaus.

[84] Athene was the goddess of spinning, but also accomplished in warfare.

[85] Achilles' spear was made from the wood of a tree felled on Mount Pelion.

[86] Cf. Sir Walter Elliot, in Jane Austen's *Persuasion* (Chapter 3), of Admiral Croft: 'Then I take it for granted,' observed Sir Walter, 'that his face is about as orange as the cuffs and capes of my livery.'

[87] Ovid is having this both ways. On the one hand, he is adopting the poet's position that to write verse about love is an alternative to having a career (see *Amores* 1.15 for another such declaration of independence); the Gothic whiteness is a mark of difference. On the other hand, this list of roles in society – a brief example of the priamel structure – puts the lover alongside these other figures, with his own uniform look. The character of the young man with a *coeur d'artichaut*, detached from the cares of the world, is a standard one in Roman comedy.

[88] Hollis raises an eyebrow at this: the hunter Orion and the shepherd Daphnis were more likely to be bronzed. Could it be that this argument works better if we think of the former as a star and the latter as a statue?

[89] The Twitard look serves to associate the lover with the night-time, and the thinness with diminished appetite. In *Amores* 1.6 the persona tries to exploit this: he's only asking the girl's janitor to open the

door wide enough to allow him in sideways: 'long love has thinned my body for the role, so that my limbs could fit into this hole.'

90 Propertius 2.34 works through this situation.

91 The poet Bion lists these examples of fidelity. Still, Ovid isn't giving his opponent all the best arguments: Phaedra, who fell in love with her stepson, is usefully rubbish.

92 Instances of *adunaton* (impossibility) – use of things that can't happen.

93 Proteus, a sea-god who can take any shape he wants, uses this power to elude Telemachus in the *Odyssey*, Book 4.

94 See *Art* 2.667ff. for praise of the older woman.

BOOK 2

1   Say 'Praise, yoohoo'; say 'praise, yoohoo' once
        more.[1]
    I've bagged the booty I was looking for.
    Hesiod and old man Homer are beneath me:
    To whom will happy lovers grant a wreath? Me.
5   Paris was no less happy when he breezed
    back home to Priam with the wife he'd seized;
    and happy Pelops won a chariot race,
    to bring you, Hippodamia, to his place.[2]
    Where are you rushing, youths? The trip I've
        planned
10   is long, and you're a distance yet from land.
    My vision brought your girl, but that won't do –
    my plan's to catch her, and retain her, too.
    If finding didn't test you, keeping will:
    the former takes good luck; the latter, skill.
15   Now urgently, Venus, and son, be near us –
    Erato, too – love's muse (your name's like Eros).
    I'm going to say how Eros finds a berth
    rather than wandering about the earth.
    The boy's a featherweight – flies where he will;
20   only tricky techniques can hold him still.[3]

    Minos managed to keep his guest from flight.
    There was one bold escape route – gaining height.

When Daedalus hid Pasiphae's disgrace
(a child, half-boy, half-bullock)[4] in a maze,
25   he pleaded, 'Send me home, Minos, most just –
I want my ashes on my native dust,
and since the fates so cruelly deny
that I can live there, still, there let me die.
Either release my son, if I am cheap,
30   or free him, if it's me you'd rather keep.'
For all he said, for all the words of woe,
and weeping, Minos wouldn't let him go.
The news hit Daedalus. So did an idea:
'My wit, and everything I need, are here!
35   While Minos holds the land and sea by right,
neither the soil, nor waves, permit our flight.
The sky remains; we'll use it if we can.
High Jupiter, grant favour to my plan.[5]
I've no desire to touch your starry seat,
40   but heavens are my one path of retreat.
Were Styx an exit, in the Styx I'd delve –
my task is now to reinvent myself.'
Need fosters genius. Who'd anticipate
that human beings could ever aviate?
45   Deploying feathers to the oars of birds,
with delicate linen as chain, he girds
the get-up round him, fixes it with glue
from melted wax, and now his labour's through.
His sparky boy studies the wings and wax,
50   not knowing father made them for their backs.
His father says, 'These boats will take us back.

We are escaping Minos by this tack.
With my device, although Minos denies
all other exits, we can broach the skies.
55   It's not for you, my boy, to work out where
we're going by Orion or the Bear.
Follow me with your wings; I'll fly before you.
Your job's to watch me; mine's to reassure you.
Now, if we go into the upper air,
60   the heat is stronger than our wax will bear,
and if we fly too low, and skim the strait,
wings become soggy wet and sag with weight.
So fly between the two – careful of gales,
but where the breezes glide, you set your sails.'
65   He shows Icarus moves, ties pinions tight
and smooths his feathers as a mother might!
he puts his own contraption on his back,
steadies his body for this novel track;
now poised, he gives his Icarus a kiss
70   and sheds tears for the country they both miss.
Atop a hill (less than a mountain's height)
they brace their bodies for a painful flight.
Daedalus moves; his son watches the oars,
and when they're off, Daedalus holds his course.
75   Icarus loves the journey. Done with caring,
he flies more stridently; his skill is daring.
(An angler thought the spectacle so odd
that his right hand released his trembling rod.)[6]
Samos is on the left (they know to follow
80   past Naxos, Paros, Delos, dear to Apollo),[7]

47

Lebinthos to the right; Calymne's wood;
Astypalaea, where the fishing's good,
and then the boy, with reckless, youthful mind
flew higher, leaving Daedalus behind.
85   The binding slid; close to the god, wax dripped;
breezes couldn't sustain his arms. He slipped.
In terror, he beheld sea from the skies,
and in his dread, darkness obscured his eyes.
Wax drizzled as his naked arms flapped on –
90   he dreaded that what held him up had gone.
He fell, and cried out, 'Daddy, I can't reach!'
and then green waters stopped his mouth from
      speech.
'Icarus!' his father cries – not father now –
'Where are you, boy? What heaven are you below?'
95   And as he cried, he saw wings on a wave.
The water has his name;[8] the earth his grave.
Though Minos couldn't check the wings of man,
I must encumber Cupid. See if I can.[9]

Those trying Thessalonian arts are dolts –
100   there's nothing magical about foreheads of colts.[10]
The grasses of Medea aren't the stuff
to mix with Marsian[11] mumblings to bring love.
Medea and Circe could have done so well
and kept their men if love stayed with a spell.
105   There's no use giving women pallid potion –
it poisons minds, and can induce commotion.
End of. Be lovable if you want love,

because a pretty face isn't enough.[12]
Are you sweet Nireus, of whom Homer writes,
110 or gentle Hylas, snatched by water sprites?[13]
Even so, to ensure your mistress won't escape,
keep mind as well as body in good shape.[14]
Beauty is fragile. As the years go by
your looks diminish; finally they die.
115 Lilies and violets don't always blow,
the rose's thorns remain when petals go,
and you, sunshine, will notice whiter hair,
as wrinkles plough your body with a share.
Enhance your beauty: feed your soul. It stays –
120 only the soul survives the funeral blaze.
Build character with liberal arts, and speak
two languages better: Latin and Greek.
Odysseus wasn't pretty, but a speaker
who made the knees of sea goddesses weaker.
125 Calypso regularly feared him going,
and told him that the sea was bad for rowing.
'Tell me about the fall of Troy!' she'd say –
each time he'd tell it in a different way.
They lingered at the seaside, where the grim
130 Rhesus' demise was her request of him.
He told the virgin (somehow she stayed pure)
the tale by sketching in the sandy shore.
'Here's Troy,' he'd say, drawing it in the sands;
'here's Simois; here my encampment stands.
135 The field's here' – here's a field – 'where Dolon
  bleeds,

who spied, and hoped to win Achilles' steeds.
Here's where King Rhesus billeted his forces;
here's where I rode back on his captured horses –'
He drew the lot; then waves came, and the camp
140   of Rhesus vanished when the sand was damp.
Calypso said, 'If I were you, I'd doubt
the waves that wiped so many heroes out.'
So there you are. Faith in the face is shoddy
and everyone needs something more than body.

145   Care and indulgence make people content –
it's roughness and aggression they resent.
We hate the hawk, who always wants a fight,
and wolves, who drive the flock away in fright.
But nobody traps swallows, which are mild,
150   and little towers keep doves out of the wild.[15]
Quarrels, be gone; out with the bitter spat;
love gently flourishes with peaceful chat.
Out, feuding wives, with husbands in pursuit –
let both think they'll eternally dispute.
155   That suits a wife, since quarrelling's her dowry –
let everything a girlfriend hears be flowery.

You're not compelled to couple by the law –
your only legislator is Amor.[16]
Bring blandishments to her; words that revive;
160   then she'll be happier when you arrive.

I have no love advice to give the rich.

If they can give, then I've nothing to teach.
Such genius, to say, whenever, 'Take me.'
They please more than my plans. They overtake
    me.
165   My vision's for the poor – I loved when poor,
and gave my songs when I could give no more.[17]
Paupers should never curse, should love with care;
they tolerate what rich men never bear.

I pulled my girlfriend's hair once, in a rage.
170   That anger, I recall, lost me an age!
I never thought I ripped her dress, but still
she said I did, so I picked up the bill.
But if you're wise, avoid my misdemeanours.
This much I know – she'll take you to the cleaners.
175   Battle's for Parthians; for girlfriends, peace,
jokes, anything that makes your love increase.[18]

If she's resistant – if you're short on charm –
persist; be obdurate. Then she'll be calm.
Follow the branch to bend it from the trunk;
180   you'll snap it if you try to be a hunk.
Swim streams by following: you'll never go
too far by breasting waves against the flow.
Following makes lions and tigers peaceful folk,
and makes the rampant bull accept the yoke.
185   Take Atalanta: who's more truculent?
Yet a deserving man made her relent.[19]
Because he found her fiendish to appease,

they say Milanion wept beneath the trees;
she made him lug her snares upon his back,

190 gave him a spear and wild boars to attack.
A centaur's arrow pierced him to the core,
but there's an arrow that's superior.
You needn't gear up for a forest trek;
you needn't schlep a snare about your neck.

195 I won't insist that your chest feels a dart:
commands are kinder by my careful art.
Yield in your contests: yielding wins the day –
assume whatever role she has you play.[20]
Approve her arguments; adopt her views:

200 say what she says; pooh-pooh what she pooh-poohs.
Laugh when she laughs. She's crying? Then you cry.
Let her decide what look is in your eye,
and, if she's playing, and she rolls a dice,
roll badly; make your move a sacrifice.

205 When playing knuckles, let her forfeit go.
Ensure you lose by throwing the worst throw.
When you're at chess, as every move goes by,
your knights, your pawns must be the ones to die.
Hold her umbrella as she goes along

210 and walk wherever she walks in the throng.
When she's on couches, prop her feet with stools;
as for those feet – fetch or remove those mules.[21]
Although you shiver, press (she'll be impressed)
her *gelida manina* to your chest.

215 It's noble, too, to hold before her sight
a mirror (this looks wrong, but feels so right).[22]

Heracles killed each fiend Hera provided,
carried the heavens where he should have resided,
then with Ionian maidens, he spun wool,
220 and, like them, fetched it by the basketful.
If Hercules obeyed his heavenly queen,
don't hesitate to be the slave he's been.
When ordered to the forum for a date,
arrive early, and be prepared to wait.
225 Dash where she says; whatever you're doing, stop it;
in case a crowd delays your journey, hop it.
She comes home from a feast – it's time for bed –
she's summoning the slave – you come instead.[23]
She's in the country? Cupid makes you work:
230 if you've no wheels, you're going to have to walk.
The dog star's heatwave can't excuse delay;
no blizzard ever seen can block your way.

Love is a type of war. Sluggards, at ease.[24]
Keep standards by the strongest strategies.
235 Night, winter, work, long marches and intense
suffering lie in Cupid's gentle tents.
You'll often bear the cold, having to lie
on naked ground, and rain dropped from the sky.[25]
We're told Apollo fed Admetus' cows
240 and hunkered down inside a bijou house.
What suited him suits you: don't show disdain
if you're eager to make romance remain.
If your straightforward, safe advance is halted
because the door in front of you is bolted,

245   then slip yourself down from an open roof;[26]
you'll find that windows, too, aren't burglar-proof.
She'll know it's her for whom you were imperilled,
and see that it's true love your gestures herald.
Leander lived without his girl – he could,
250   but swam to see her; then she understood.
And never patronise her senior aides –
not even menials – serving boys and maids:
kindness costs nothing. Greet them all by name;
shake all their hands; treat everyone the same.
255   If slaves touch you for gifts on Fortune Day,
then dole them out – it isn't much to pay.
Honour that day when maids saved Roman lives,
offering themselves to Gauls, dressed up as wives.[27]
Trust me – rely on plebs: the janitor,
260   and then, the one who guards the inner door.
When giving gifts, don't spend a vast amount:
be clever – then the thought can really count.
The fields are rich; begin with swelling fruit –
then have a boy deliver rustic loot:
265   though you can say it's from your private park, it
was really produce from the farmer's market.
Give grapes, or give her chestnuts. (Amaryllis
craved nuts, now doesn't. How changing her will is.)
Why not dispatch a field thrush or a dove
270   to her as a reminder of your love?
(Some with the recipients death, or bereft old
     age.
I hope they die, who make gifts sacrilege.)

Are poems something you should send along?
No, no – there's not much honour for a song.

275 Poems win praise, for sure, but there's a hitch –
she'll want real gifts. Barbarians charm, if rich.
Today we're living in an age of gold:
love is for sale; honours are bought and sold.
Homer could bring all nine Muses to Rome,
280 but if that's all you brought, Homer, go home.
There is a clique of female cognoscenti,
and girls who want to be like that, aplenty.
Praise poetry should work with either crowd
if you're seductive reading it aloud.
285 Give them the dedication: then they've got
a kind of gift, whether they're smart or not.

What's useful, that you're just about to do?
Contrive it so your mistress begs you to.
Is freedom promised to a slave of yours?
290 Then see that it's your girlfriend he implores.
If you'd let off a slave, or let him go,
ensure that it's not you, but her he'll owe.
You get to benefit, she gets to give;
you lose nothing; she plays the executive.

295 If you're concerned to keep her, it's your duty
to make her think you're gobsmacked by her
          beauty.
If she's rocking a Coan dress, admire

the Coan style; if Tyrian, you love Tyre.
You love gold dresses, but she glisters more.

300   Is she in mohair? Mohair you adore.
She's standing in her slip? Exclaim – be bold –
'Girl, I'm on fire!' then, coyly, 'Aren't you cold?'
She parts her hair? Then partings are so her.
She wrenches it with tongs? Then lucky hair.

305   Applaud her when she sings, or hits the floor,
and if she stops, say that you wanted more.[28]
Even in bed, say what she's doing right,
and what pleasures you have with her at night.
If she's more violent than crazed Medusa,

310   make out that she's as smooth as her seducer,
only, never reveal that you misled:
a false look can dismantle what you said.
Art works when hidden; being caught brings shame –
her faith in you will never be the same.

315   Often in autumn – what season's more fine? –
when grapes are full and blush with purple wine,
when cold descends, and heat dissolves the chill –
in this uncertain climate, we get ill.
All health to her, but if she takes to bed –

320   if the unreliable sky goes to her head –
then let your love and your devotion show:
what you plant now, your sickle soon will mow.
Don't be disgusted by her foul disease,
but be the one who brings her remedies;

325   kisses won't tire her; let her see you cry –

let lips absorb your tears when they are dry.
Pray vocally; as often as it seems
to please her, tell her of your happy dreams.
Let an old maid cleanse bed and bedroom and
330   bring eggs and sulphur in her trembling hand.
Traces of welcome care lie in these skills –
you're on a path that often leads to wills.
But don't let anything vex your Camille:
your manner should be one of charming zeal.
335   Don't starve her; don't you bring the medicine cup;
prescriptions are for rivals to make up.

Still, setting sail requires a different breeze
from when you've reached the middle of your seas.
When love's beginning, practice makes it stronger;
340   by feeding it, you help your love last longer.
The bull you fear now wasn't always big;
the tree that shelters you was once a twig;
streams are born little; as they flow, they grow
and gather waters wherever they go.
345   Let her grow used to you: nothing does more
than habit: get it. Nothing is a bore.
Within her ears and eyes, take pride of place –
night, day, make her accustomed to your face.
When you're more confident that you can leave her,
350   and when a trip away's likely to grieve her,
give her a rest. Fields, rested, yield more grain,
and dry earth can absorb heavenly rain:
Phyllis burned mildly for Demophoön

when he was near, but blazed when he was gone;
355   Odysseus' absence racked Penelope;
Laodamia missed the man she couldn't see.
But keep your absence brief: soon she'll calm down;
the missing man fades when new love's in town:
When Menelaus goes, who takes his place?
360   Helen accepts her guest's tepid embrace.
You left them, Menelaus – you're the goof
whose wife and guest were under the same roof.
You'd give a hawk some timid doves to keep
or leave a wolf on mountains full of sheep.
365   It wasn't Helen's error, or the man's –
he did what you'd have done, given the chance.
You gave adultery a time and place;
Paris did Helen only by your grace.
Her bed was solitary; she was distressed
370   and then in came a reconstructed guest.
A gentleman had her. What could she do?
She is absolved. Menelaus, I blame you.

More terrifying than the russet boar
who twists wild dogs within his lightning jaw,
375   or lionesses giving cubs a teat,
than little vipers hurt by careless feet,
is she who finds a rival in her bed.
Her scorching face reveals a mind to dread:
She is possessed, reaches for sword and flame
380   and, touched by Bacchus' horns, loses her shame.
Medea, when her husband broke his oath

punished him through her sons, killing them both;
the swallow, too 's a parent to abhor –
you notice that her chest's spattered with gore.[29]
385   The cautious man is wary of these slips:
they wreck the firmest, best relationships.
Not that my censures tie you to one woman.
New brides don't even get that – it's not human.
Play, but be sneaky; shy – don't get found out –
390   this kind of crime's nothing to brag about.
Don't give to one woman the other's gifts;
don't keep your lechery within fixed shifts;
have more than one retreat where you can go,
in case you use a hiding place she'll know.
395   When writing notes, check you've concealed your
        tracks –
many a note's been read through unwiped wax.[30]
When she's impugned, Venus declares jihad,
turns arms back, giving you the grief she had:
King Agamemnon used to stick to one:
400   his wife. He strayed, and then he was undone.
She heard of Chryses' daughter; came to learn
how he prayed vainly for her safe return;
she heard who ended up with Briseis
(who changed hands, lengthening hostilities).
405   She heard all that; Cassandra, though, she saw:
the king was prized now by the prize he bore.
That's when she took Aegisthus to her bed,
and her revenge was – Agamemnon dead.[31]

If deeds that you've concealed still come to light,
410   dismiss even the blatant things outright.
Don't become abject; don't be overkind:
that's indication of a guilty mind.
There's one way of assuaging everything:
good sex can contradict the previous fling.
415   Some witches favour savory, noxious plants.
I think they're poisonous – why take the chance?
Or pepper mixed with seed of stinging nettle,
or wine infused with camomile's blond petal;
Venus, served on Eryx's shady hills,[32]
420   won't let these pharmacists induce her thrills.
Go for white Megaran onions; what plant matches
rocket, growing in most vegetable patches?
Eggs, too, are good; Hymettian honey's fine,
as are the nuts that come from prickly pine.

425   Love Muse, why hold us up with magic art?[33]
My chariot should be heading for the heart.
Just now I urged discretion; still, sometimes
change tack: I say, reveal your secret crimes.
Don't knock this inconsistency: one breeze
430   alone won't take a crew across the seas.
Now Thracian north, now south-east keeps us
       going;
sails fill when Zephyrus, or the south is blowing;
and note how charioteers race round their courses:
they might relax the reins, or hold their horses.
435   You feebly pamper some to no avail –

if no rival's around, love can grow stale.
Characters languish if their lot is kind;
comfort's a burden to the balanced mind.
Just as a fire will gradually abate,
440 then hide as white ash settles in the grate,
still, with a little sulphur, dead flame burns,
and all the light there was before returns:
so, when freedom from care turns feelings flaccid,
you should revive love with a dash of acid.
445 Make her afraid; reheat her tepid mind;
let her blanch at some evidence she'll find;
four-plus times happy is the man for whom
an injured, grieving woman will succumb:
who, when her stubborn ears hear these complaints,
450 loses her voice and colouring, then faints.[34]
I long to be the one for whom she'll tear
her cheeks with nails; for whom she'll rip her hair;
at whom she looks with weeping, rolling eyes –
for whom (although she'd rather not) she dies.
455 And if you want a break, then keep it brief,
in case the wait makes rage out of her grief;
in time, her lily neck will feel you wrap
your arms around it; take her on your lap.
She weeps; give kisses, and the joys of passion.
460 There will be peace. Rage passes in this fashion.
She foams? She's hostile? Then be reconciled
by treaties 'tween the sheets, and she'll be mild.
There Concord dwells, unarmed. That very place,
believe me, is the breeding ground of Grace.

465 Doves who have finished fighting quickly speak
in flattering coos, and snuggle beak to beak.

In the beginning, matter had no order:
between earth, sea and stars, there was no border;
soon sky landed on land, the waters grew
470 around the earth; chaotic void withdrew;
the air took birds; woods hosted animals
and deep under the water lurked the shoals.
The human race then roamed the lonely plain;
they had coarse bodies, and more brawn than
brain.
475 Woods were their home, their food grass, leaves
their beds;
companionship never entered their heads.
Seductive lust softened the stubborn mind
when, in one place, woman and man combined.
They didn't need some teacher's scholarship
480 to do their business; Venus gave no tip.
Birds have their lovers, and the lady fish
can join their joys with whomever they wish;
snakes tangle up with snakes, doe follows buck;
dogs go out dogging, and they don't need luck;
485 the glad ewe frisks; bulls drive a heifer silly;
the snub-nosed nanny goat supports rough billy.
Deterred neither by distance or by floods,
beside themselves, mares race after their studs.
So go – take angry girls this heady potion,
490 for only this will ease their wild commotion.

It's better than the drugs doled out at Troy,
and helps sinners regain their former joy.[35]

I just wrote that, then saw Apollo come
to pluck his golden lyre with his thumb.[36]
495 Laurel was in his hand; his holy hair
was laureate; the bard was really there.
'Lascivious teacher – make your students follow
instead towards the temples of Apollo.
Upon its walls, a world famous inscription
500 says, "Know yourself." Let that be your prescription.
Only self-knowing souls will wisely love,
because they find their own skills are enough.
A lovely face is made to please beholders,
and if your colour's good, then show your
     shoulders.
505 Avoid silence if talking is your thing,
but if it's drinking, drink; if singing, sing.
In chats, though, orators must not rehearse
their speeches, nor mad poets declaim their verse.'
Apollo spoke. Apollo must be heard,
510 and total faith placed in his holy word.

So, back to basics. If a lover's wise,
he'll win, and gain his goal, by my advice.
Not all furloughs have dividends to pay;
not all winds help a boat that's lost its way.
515 There are small joys, but rather more gives pain,
and so prepare your mind to take the strain.

Countless as Athos' hares, or Hybla's bees,
countless as berries in Athene's trees,
or shells on shores, are griefs that love can bring.
520   We suffer from the poison in the sting.
You saw her in, but you've been told she's out.
In that case, it's your eyes you have to doubt.
The door's shut on a night she asked you round?
Then don't give up – lie on the dirty ground,
525   and if a lying, self-important nurse
should ask, 'Why does that man besiege our doors?'
flatter the door and her whom it encloses
by placing on its post your crown of roses.
Come when she wants; go when she wants no more:
530   a gentleman should never be a bore.
Instinct is sometimes right. She shouldn't say,
'When will this person ever go away?'
And don't think it's accursed to let her beat
you; it's not wrong to kiss her tender feet.

535   I dally in small things; my soul should start
to sing big. Crowd, join me with all your heart.
It will be tough, but then, all good things will:
hard labour is demanded by our skill.
Put up with rivals – victory will be yours –
540   like a victorious consul, take the applause.
I didn't say this – it's the oak of Zeus:[37]
no other tips of mine will be more use.
She winks? So what. She writes? Don't touch the
      letter.

She wants to come? She can. She's going? Let her.
545 A husband does this for his lawful spouse
whenever gentle, helpful sleep allows.
In this, I should confess, I've sometimes erred.
What can I say? I'm less good than my word.
If someone winks at my companion,
550 am I OK? No anger spurs me on?
My girlfriend's fellow kissed her. I complained.
The problem is, my love is unrestrained.
It's harmed me more than once. A wiser chap
accommodates, so others spot the gap.
555 Not knowing's good; let her conceal caresses
lest she become shameless when she confesses.
Young men, remember that you shouldn't pry –
let sinners think they've given you the lie.
Love grows when busted; fate afflicts a pair
560 who can continue in what laid them bare.
Throughout the skies, they tell the story where
Vulcan caught Mars and Venus in a snare.
A passion bowled paternal Mars right over
and changed grim warlord into callow lover;
565 She heard his prayers (heaven has no safer bet);
no country wife, she isn't hard to get.
The minx would mock her husband's feet, and smirk
about his hands, hardened by fire and work.
She'd mimic Vulcan for the god of war:
570 charm, mixed with beauty, gave her something more.
They covered up their assignations well,
but soon they blushed at their *crime passionnel*.

Daylight exposed it – who can dupe the sun? –
and Vulcan realised what his wife had done.
575　(O Sun you're a disgrace. Seek a reward
for silence – something she can well afford.)
Over and round the bed, Vulcan could strap
nooses, so dark that no one saw the trap.
He says he's off to Lemnos; lovers meet,
580　and ping: they're both chained, naked to the sheet.
He calls the gods; the captives are on show –
Venus can barely make her tears not flow.
Caught in the snare, they couldn't hide their faces
or put their hands over their special places.
585　One jeered, 'Oh mighty Mars, if it's a strain,
then I would cheerfully take on your chain!'
Neptune begrudgingly removed the brace,
and Venus went to Paphos, Mars to Thrace.
Vulcan, look what you did – what carried on
590　in secret's open now that shame has gone.
You say you screwed up now, it drives you mad,
and you repent of all the skill you had.
Don't you behave like this, because it's heinous
to set the sort of trap that captured Venus.
595　Don't try and spring a rival into fetters;
don't fish out hidden meanings in her letters.
If these things are worth catching, catch them when
water and fire have made you married men.[38]
No dames in long skirts: as I've said before,
600　let's keep to fun permitted by the law.

Who blabs of Ceres to the populace?[39]
Or divulges the rites of Samothrace?
Silence is a small virtue; a great vice
is saying things you shouldn't publicise.
605   It's right that gabby Tantalus should clutch
at apples fruitlessly – that he should parch.[40]
Venus insists that nobody should speak
of her rites – leave them if you like to leak.
Even if her mystery objects don't belong
610   in chests – if her priests bang no warning gong,
still, since her rites are practised all around,
we must observe them where we can't be found.

When she undresses, Venus has to stand
modestly, covering pubes with her left hand.
615   Beasts mate *al fresco*, all over the place –
a girl who sees this needs to turn her face.
Boudoirs and bolts assist our furtive arts,
just as our clothes cover our private parts.
If there's no shadow, then we have to seek
620   perspicuous gloom, or less than daylight's peak.
Before roofing kept sunshine out, and showers –
when food and shelter came from the oak-tree's
     bowers –
sex happened in a grove or in a cave;
primitive people bothered to behave.
625   In modern times we seek fame from a shag,
and all we're after is the power to brag.
You probe women wherever and, what's sadder,

67

it's simply so that you can say, 'I've had her.'
Is there no shortage of the girls you handle,
630   then point at, offering some tale of scandal?
Worse; some fake what, if true, they can't accept –
claim that there's none with whom they haven't
    slept.
If they can't have the bodies then they clutch
at names, and shame people they didn't touch.[41]
635   So put a hundred bolts upon girls' doors
and shut them up, you baleful janitors.
What's safe now, if adulterers can claim
what didn't happen, and besmirch a name?
Me, though, I hardly ever kiss and tell –
640   my mystic pleasures are protected well.

Above all, don't tell women of their flaws:
men often find a lie can help their cause.
Swift Perseus found no reason for rejection
in his lovely Andromeda's complexion;
645   Andromache's stature made men reject her:
one man thought her just right, and he was Hector.
What you don't like, get used to, and forgive:
age tempers much; young love is sensitive.
While branches quicken in their greeny sap,
650   winds can dislodge them with the faintest tap,
but soon, hardened by time, the tree can take
the winds, bear fruit, and still the bough won't
    break.
Daily, time softens each physical flaw –

what was a weakness won't be any more.
655 People with nervous nostrils can abide,
before too long, the noisome ox's hide.
Where you find fault, words can bring beauty back:
people say 'dusky' when they're meaning black.
'Venus' means cross-eyed, and 'Minerva's grey,
660 while 'willowy' can mean, wasting away.
'Petite' is short. Say 'curvy' if she's fat.
What's most like her, but good? Then call her that.

Don't ask her age, or who was head of state
when she was born (let censors keep the date),[42]
665 especially if her youth has passed, bloom fled
and now she plucks white hairs out of her head.
This is an age (or later) youths should know –
the field is fruitful; it's a field to sow.
Accept the task, while strength and years permit,
670 before old age pads up to finish it.
So plough the soil with shares, or seas with oars
or throw your muscle into bloody wars,
or give to women strength, body and care:
you need the same tactics and power there.
675 What's more, they have more prudence in these
       things;
only they have technique experience brings.
They compensate with knowledge of the world
and take some trouble not to seem so old,
so you can choose one from a thousand ways
680 to have sex – more than any book displays.[43]

They do not need provoking to their pleasure –
woman and man feel joy in equal measure.
I hate sex when it brings uneven joys:
that's why I don't like doing it with boys,

685   or girls who give out, thinking it a bind;
they're dry, and spinning wool is on their mind:
sex out of duty is unwelcome sport –
let no girl please me, feeling that she ought.[44]
I love them to express delight, and say

690   that I should keep on, that I should delay;
I love to see her crazed with conquered eyes
or languishing from contact she denies.
These are the benefits nature deprives
from most, except the over-thirty-fives.

695   Let those who want to rush drink Beaujolais –
pour me the wine that's long been put away.
Plane trees can take the sun when they mature
and meadows freshly grown make bare feet sore.
Between Hermione, or Helen, her mother,

700   Medusa or her mum, whom would you rather?[45]
If you prefer a rapture that's matured,
keep at it, and you'll win a fine reward.

Two lovers are in bed. The bed's aware;
the bedroom's doors are shut. Muse, linger where,

705   without you, they dissert of their accord,
neither are either of their left hands bored;
fingers find what to do in secret parts,
where Cupid slyly tingles with his darts.

So strongest Hector satisfied his wife –
710　war wasn't the sole object of his life –
Achilles, too, and captured Briseis
pressed sheets like this when he left war for peace.
Briseis, how did it feel to be beneath
those hands, blooded always with Phrygian death?
715　Did it meet your lascivious demands
that your limbs came to those victorious hands?
Don't hurry love, I say with confidence –
elicit it, delay it, sense by sense.
When you discover spots that give her such
720　delight, then let no shame deter your touch:
you'll see her eyes flash with a tremulous gleam,
as when the sun flicks waters with its beam;
moans will arise, and then a friendly purr,
and sweet sighs, joking words unique to her.
725　But don't leave her, flaunting your bigger sails –
it's not a race where one of you prevails –
no, rush together to the line – it's sweet
for man and woman, both equally beat.
This is the ideal pace, at least, when leisure
730　allows; if fear's not rushing secret pleasure – [46]
in which case, ply the oars – you're not secure
to wait – goad bolting horses with a spur.

So, grateful young people, let's leave it there:
bring palms, bring myrtle to my perfumed hair.
735　The doctor to the Greeks was Podalarius,
Achilles, strong, had skill, Nestor was serious,

Calches read entrails, Ajax wielded arms,
Automedon could race. I know love's charms.
Call me a prophet, young men, sing my praise;
740   let my name be proclaimed in every place.
As Vulcan gave Achilles weapons, so
I give you these. Conquer wherever you go;
but if you trounce an Amazon with my sword,
mark on the spoils that *Ovid was your lord.*

745   Oh – now sweet women ask what they can learn.
All right – you are my schedule's next concern.

NOTES

1. Shouts of triumph. The cry given to Bacchus – *evoe* – is also written *euhoe*.

2. Pelops, the founder of the dynasty that produced Agamemnon and Menelaus, won Hippodamia by cheating in a chariot race.

3. Another example of Ovid's ingenious sophistry: it was Eros' youth and smallness that made his power seem so negligible to the poet at the start of Book 1; now it is what gives Eros the advantage.

4. As at *Art* 1.326.

5. The language here, echoing Virgil's invocation to Augustus at the beginning of the *Georgics*, serves to draw an analogy between Daedalus' powers of invention and the poet's.

6. This cameo anticipates Auden's treatment of the subject, 'Musée des Beaux Arts', in which the tragedy blends in with daily life.

7. Green (pp. 364–6) offers a detailed discussion of Ovid's erratic geography here.

8. The Icarian Sea, named after him. (Green offers other possibilities.)

9. This whole episode has been clearly introduced, and rounded off in the same spirit; but the episode could have been dealt with in a couple of lines – a simile rather than a narrative. But Ovid has turned it into a tale that is by turns charming and pathetic. Why? Hollis in *Ovid*, ed. J. W. Binns (Routledge, 1973) considers these digressions to be 'testing ground for the *Metamorphoses*' and points out that a version of this myth appears in the longer poem. But is there anything more to it than that? Perhaps. Even on the level of what Ovid is teaching, there is some instructive value: young people should listen to wiser heads. (The reader is often addressed as *iuvenis* – a young man.)

   It's possible to go further though, and to take something from this about how Ovid is doing the teaching. In the didactic tradition, the poet must assert his own unique understanding of the subject. Just as, at the beginning of Book 1, Ovid explained that he wasn't leaning on the knowledge of Hesiod, but rather on his own experience, so here he shows Daedalus taking paths out of problems that had not been anticipated. That moment of inspiration Daedalus has is what we might now call 'genius': Ovid calls it *ingenium*, a quality he ascribes elsewhere to a certain kind of inspired poet (*Amores* 1.15) whose skill goes beyond facility with verse (which Ovid has called *ars* in that earlier poem). It's worth noting, too, that Daedalus' device is called a labour of art. Daedalus appears here as an all-round creator – a man who can build mazes and find ways around them. In this passage, at least, he is analogous to the artist in a way that anticipates James Joyce's use of him: here, too, he has the spirit of the poet.

10 This is the part of a foal's forehead that a mare bites off at birth.

11 Marsi, in Italy, was associated with magic.

12 Be lovable – a proposition both simple and challenging; but tips on how to meet the challenge follow.

13 Two examples of the mythically beautiful man.

14 Juvenal's Satire 10 culminates memorably with similar advice: abandon vanity; your goal should be *mens sana in corpore sano*. Ovid can find much to admire about the endurance of character (2.668ff.; 3.565ff.), while also warning about fugitive good looks (3.59ff.).

15 There are traces here of Ovid's singular perspective on the Roman dream: rather than looking back to a better age when men and women were hardier, he celebrates progress and pampering. See on cultivation/culture, both in Book 3 below, and *Treatments*.

16 Cf. Joni Mitchell: 'We don't need no piece of paper from the City Hall.' But this was a risky sentiment to express. Augustus' reforms made those pieces of paper desirable. The law against adultery was just one of the laws he passed in 18 BC. Another was designed to encourage wedlock: unmarried or childless men aged between twenty-five and sixty, and women in the same situation aged between twenty and fifty, stood to lose their inheritance rights. The law was hugely unpopular, and Augustus ended up having to soften it. This, and the fact that we have no evidence of it being enforced, could explain why Ovid is being more forthright (for him).

[17] See note on 1.729 (note 87) on how a lover's lack of ambition beyond being a lover makes his slacking a vocation in its own right. The gift of poetry is a commonplace in elegy: both Propertius and Tibullus offer poems, and argue for their value (see the dedication). In Ovid's bitter poem about the madame, she offends the poet most when she is overheard to advise the trainee bawd to snub a suitor who has nothing more than writing to offer.

[18] These lines sit delicately between the passages above and below them: they are linked tenuously to the argument about money by the suggestion that rough, bullying behaviour can be expensive. As a result, the poet proposes a different course.

[19] Atalanta decided that she would only marry a man who could outrun her. She killed men who failed in the attempt. But Milanion beat her – he delayed her by strewing golden apples in her way. (He'd been given a head start, as if he were prey.)

[20] Later, women will hear that they shouldn't take winning too seriously (3.371–80).

[21] Literally, slippers.

[22] Ovid stresses this because it would have seemed demeaning to a Roman man; this was the job of a female slave.

[23] In case the mirror task did not seem humiliating enough, the man must now answer as the slave. The idea of love turning men into slaves is an elegiac trope: the first lines of Propertius' *oeuvre* express definitively the 'servitude of love'. In Ovid's context, this becomes less a psychological predicament, and more a ploy.

[24] Ovid continues to remind us that the path of love is hard as he moves from love's servitude (the *servitium amoris*) to the traditional analogy with warfare (*militia amoris*). Ovid's Amores 1.9 sets up the recruiting stall. Here the tone has the brusqueness of some recent Maybelline campaigns – for example, 'When you're in the field, you shouldn't have to worry about your makeup. New active combat colours / They won't run, so you won't have to either.'

[25] The first reference in the poem to the *paraklausithyron* – the stock scene of Roman comedy and elegy, in which the lover is locked out

of the girl's house, and must plead with the doorman. The tradition is that the lover spends the night on the beloved's doorstep. It can also be the setting for fights between rival men.

[26] The ingress here would be a hole in the roof, normal in townhouses. It was called the *compluvium*, and it would allow rain to fall into a small inner pool.

[27] Two examples of days on which slaves are held in honour. Fortune Day was around the midsummer solstice. On 'Maids' Day', women sacrificed to Juno as a tribute to the maids who took the place of their mistresses when Gauls demanded Roman women. Not only did the maids act as substitutes, but also tipped the Romans off on the best time to attack.

[28] The flipside of this advice appears at *Cures* 331ff.

[29] Procne killed her children in rage at her husband Tereus. She turned into a swallow.

[30] Wax tablets were reusable, and functioned as jotters. As a result, there was a risk that the last thing someone wrote on it could still be showing. Cf. *Art* 3.495. It reminds me of an anecdote I've been unable to trace, about an Oxford don who suspected his wife of having an affair, but needed to visit the Post Office shortly after she'd been there if he was to prove it. The lover's address was imprinted in mirror writing on the blotting paper. (Cf. Michael Frayn, *Spies*.)

[31] This is the plot of Aeschylus' tragedy *Agamemnon*, with some back story from *Iliad*, Book 1 added. Agamemnon kept Chryseis as a spoil of war; her father brought a plague upon the Greeks until the girl was returned. In her place, Aeschylus took Briseis from Achilles. As a result, Achilles refused to fight, and so made the Trojan War last longer. Agamemnon later took up with the seer Cassandra. Ovid here emphasises her appearance as a factor in Agamemnon's death at the hands of his wife Clytemnestra.

[32] Venus' temple in the shade of Mount Eryx in Sicily was served by sacred prostitutes.

[33] A fair question. Ovid might reasonably blame an external agency

for this digression. Why is this the time to talk about aphrodisiacs? Perhaps because they would be useful if the love student needs to have the kind of sex that conceals the fact that he's had other sex. Two clues from *Cures* could point us in this direction: l. 402 (have sex with someone else before having sex with the woman in whom you're trying to lose interest) and l. 797 (onions can prime you for sex, so don't eat them). So here's how not to do the thing you'd want to do if you want the relationship to end.

³⁴ A debt to Tibullus (1.10.63–4): 'four times happy the guy / at whose chagrin a gentle girl can cry.'

³⁵ The digressions have been so rapid and varied that we might need reminding that, by the end of this passage, Ovid is still talking about band-aid sex. So why does it take a whole journey back to the creation of the world? This is a parody of Lucretius, whose *On the Nature of Things* includes descriptions of the universe. It's odd for Ovid to draw some comfort from our resemblance to beasts: although he's fond of animal comparisons (even fonder of them when he's referring to women), his position is often that of a man pleased by progress and evolution. But Hollis points to two lines in particular of Lucretius (5.1017-18): 'Sex weakened humans, and the young applied / their charms to take apart their parents' pride.' With this link in place, we can see sex as the agency that has brought mankind to the civilised state of which he approves.

³⁶ Apollo appears here as the sober-sides deity, who restores Ovid from his waywardness. Although Ovid said at the outset of *Art* that his precepts don't come from Apollo, one can see that the god's interruption now comes at the moment when the poet is preoccupied with medicine. Apollo is the god of healing, which is in this case sexual.

³⁷ A reference to Zeus' oracle at Dodona.

³⁸ When a bride crosses the threshold of her new home, the groom gives her a torch and a jug, to symbolise her new duties of cooking and cleaning. This affirmation of marriage isn't Ovid's subtlest piece of gliding around the censor; but he is perhaps in danger of being

too convincing about the hazards of dealing with adulterers. His authority for the story of Venus and Mars is the highest: Homer (*Odyssey*, Book 8).

[39] The Eleusinian mysteries were shared by members of Ceres' cult.

[40] One story that accounts for Tantalus' punishment is that he betrayed secrets he'd heard during his regular banquets on Mount Olympus.

[41] Cf. Chaucer, *The House of Fame*, 3.1758–1762. 'For goddes love, that sit above,/Thogh we may not the body have/Of wimmen, yet, so god yow save!/Let men glewe on us the name;/Suffyceth that we han the fame.'

[42] The passage in praise of the older woman anticipates the passage in praise of the older man at *Art* 3.565. But some textual problems with the later passage make this praise for the older man ambiguous. Based on the analogy with this passage, can we clear up those ambiguities by seeing this parallel? Or should we be cautious, aware as we are that Ovid equivocates?

[43] This translation suggests something like the work of Dr Alex Comfort, with diagrams. John R. Clarke writes of the word *tabella* (picture, *tableau*), 'Ovid puts the erotic *tabella* into the picture gallery; the context is that of the man of taste looking at high art.'

[44] These lines are of perhaps more interest for what they contribute to the debate about pleasure than the passing reference to homosexuality. At least, a Roman reader would not have thought the reference to same-sex coupling too odd. But Ovid's discussion of it is revealing. As far as he was concerned, the physical pleasure in this style of congress would have been unequal; the penetrator would have derived all the pleasure, and his companion would have suffered the indignity of being penetrated; the former would have been on top in two senses.

More relevant to Ovid's readers, in his time and perhaps in ours, is the question of whether the woman's pleasure is important to the man because he wants her to be happy, or because he wants to exult in his own power to please. Some find the imparity of the experience underscored by the fact that male pleasure is the subject of two books, and female pleasure of one (e.g. John Henderson in Gibson and Sharrock, p. 77ff.). The need for the male ego to delight in the sadness he can cause suggests this is likely, and the present passage is open to the most subjective interpretation. But, given the scandalised discussions of female desire elsewhere – for example, the derided figure of Claudius' wife Messalina (as in Juvenal's 6th Satire and, more scientifically, in Pliny's *Natural History* 10.83) – the casual, untroubled way in which Ovid can entertain the idea of these impulses as natural is refreshing.

45 The genius of this rhetorical trick lies in its simplicity: he points to the most beautiful woman imaginable, to say that her daughter must have been less beautiful; and then the ugliest, to say that the mother must have been more beautiful. Ovid is inviting us to laugh as much at his technique as at the argument he's advancing.

46 Cf. the Woody Allen character in *Everything You Ever Wanted to Know about Sex . . .* who discovers that his beloved is aroused only by the fear of being caught.

BOOK 3

1   I armed Greeks against Amazons, but here's
an arsenal for you Penthesileas.[1]
So now let a more balanced fight begin –
Venus' and Cupid's favourites can win.

5   Armed men can't fairly rival naked girls.
Men, such a victory would make you churls.
Somebody in the audience[2] asks, 'Why stock
vipers with poisons, or hand wolves a flock?'
The lapses of a few girls shouldn't blight

10   the whole sex; judge each one in her own right.
So if the sons of Atreus could list a
charge sheet against both Helen and her sister –[3]
if it was Eriphyle's love of gold
that sent her husband (live) to the underworld –[4]

15   then there's Penelope, whose man spent ten
years fighting; ten more wandering back again;
and Laodamia, widowed, who went
to find her man before her years were spent;
and then Alcestis, whom Admetus wed,

20   accepted his fate – death took her instead.[5]
'Take me, Capareus – let's mix ash,' exclaims
Evadne as she jumps into his flames.
Virtue's own name is feminine in gender,
as is her dress – her flock's quick to defend her.

25 These aren't the minds, though, that demand my
  craft –
  I need but small sails for my little raft.
  Lewd women only – none of the above:
  I'll show how women ought to take their love.
  Women don't wield torches or scary bows –
30 I seldom see men suffer from their blows.[6]
  Look at the evidence: men often cheat –
  few gentle girls are guilty of deceit:
  Medea had babies.[7] Jason pulled the plug
  the moment someone else gave him a hug.
35 When you left her, Theseus, for all you knew,
  Ariadne was for waterbirds to chew.
  There is a place called Nine Ways (as it still is)
  where trees weep leaves for their abandoned Phyllis.
  Aeneas, famed for piety, was your guest,
40 Dido – he's why a sword sent you to rest.[8]
  What lost you all? I'll tell you: love can kill.
  You lack the knack. Keep love alive with skill.

  And still you wouldn't know! But Venus landed
  before my eyes, and now I am commanded.
45 She said, 'Do girls really deserve it, when
  they're all defenceless, facing armoured men?
  They have two books, telling them what to do.
  The other side needs educating too;
  and Stesichorus, who called Helen cur,
50 sang with a luckier lyre when praising her.[9]
  If I know you, you wouldn't want to offend

smart girls; winning their grace should be your end.'
She spoke, and, from the myrtle in her hair,
she had some berries and a leaf to spare;
55 I took them, sensed her power, saw the sky
glow purely, felt my bosom's burdens fly.
So learn my precepts, girls, while I've the wit –
if modesty, or laws, or rights, permit.

Remember that old age arrives in haste –
60 no time that flees from you will go to waste.
Play while you can. Enjoy what you still say
is vernal youth – like streams, years trickle away.
The wave that passes won't be back again,
the time that passes you cannot regain.
65 Youth is for using; soon, though, it'll run –
nothing that follows it will be as fun.
I saw those stalks as violets, fully blown,
and from those thorns I had a rosy crown.
In time, you too, who once rejected lovers,
70 will lie, a cold old maid, in lonely covers,
no nightly fighting breaking down your door,
no morning roses scattered on the floor.
How quickly wrinkles wilt the body's frame;
lost is the hue that set a face aflame.
75 The white shocks you protest were always there
sprout suddenly throughout a head of hair.
A snake sloughs off his years when skin is shed;
age leaves a stag when antlers leave his head.
Our age comes with no profit. Pluck the bud

80   which, if it goes unplucked, falls with a thud.
       Besides, you make youth shorter if you yield
       children. Continual harvests age a field.[10]

       Endymion brought no blushes to the moon;[11]
       Aurora wasn't awkward with her boon.
85   Although Adonis' death made Venus mourn,
       still, how were Harmony and Aeneas born?
       These goddesses' examples should inspire you
       not to withhold your joys if men desire you.
       Men cheat, but do you lose? No – joys remain.
90   Nothing is gone, however much men gain.
       Though flints erode, and iron shrinks with wear,
       there's no fear that you'll harm yourself down
          there.
       Who'd stop flames lighting other flames? Who'd
          keep
       all the vast waters in the gaping deep?
95   And yet women tell men, 'But there's no use.'
       Except for bath water, what can you lose?[12]
       My arguments don't take you for a bawd –[13]
       but fears are vain – your capital's insured.
       I'll drift more when some stronger forces blow:
100   we're still in port. One breeze, and off we go.

       First, then, couture.[14] In cultivated land
       crops grow; grapes grow with viticulture's hand.
       Beauty's a gift from God. How many of you
       can boast of it? The answer's: very few.[15]

105   Look after looks. Neglected looks will fade,
even if you're Venus in Mount Ida's shade.
Women in past times didn't cultivate
their looks,[16] but couldn't get a cultured mate.
The tunic of Andromache's hard-wearing –
110   her husband has a military bearing.
You should dress up to be Ajax's bride –
his shield was made of seven oxen's hide.
Simple and crude worked then; now Rome is gold,
and has the riches of the conquered world.
115   Compare the Capitol's shrines to what they were:
you'll say they're for a different Jupiter.
No senate house could suit our senate more;[17]
when Tatius ruled, though, it was made of straw.
The Palatine boasts lords and Phoebus now –[18]
120   before, though, it was pasture for the plough.
Others like days of old. For what it's worth,
it suits my style to have a later birth,
not for the mining of gold's stubborn ore,
nor for the pearls plucked out of every shore,
125   nor as the quarries turn mountains to caves,
and building projects take the place of waves,[19]
but for the culture: crudeness that lived on
until our grandfathers, at last has gone.

Now, women, please be careful not to stretch
130   your ears with stones Ind's murky waters fetch;
nor come weighed down by clothes woven with gold,
hoping to turn us on – it leaves us cold.[20]

We like you smart: don't have unruly hair –
it just takes pats to ruin or repair.
135 There's more than one style: go for one that's you
(and check mirrors to make sure it'll do).
Long heads need central partings – nothing more.
That is the style Laodamia wore.
Show ears, if it's a round face that you've got,
140 and at your crown, fasten a little knot.
Some let it lie on shoulders: it's the look
Phoebus Apollo of the sweet lyre took.
Some tie it up in girdled Diana's way
(she'd wear it thus when scaring savage prey);
145 one looks good with a loosely packed bouffant,
while tightly bound hair is what others want.
A tortoise-shell comb makes some hair behave,
while other hair stays floaty like a wave.
Perhaps as many acorns fall from trees;
150 go counting alpine beasts, or Hyblan bees.
There is no way to cover all the range,
especially since, every day, they change.
Some hair can seem ignored since yesterday:
it's just been combed! It's meant to look that way.
155 Art looks like life: Iole was a scruff
when Hercules said, 'She's the one I love.'
Abandoned Ariadne was the same
when Bacchus' car and whooping Bacchants came.

Nature's kinder to women than to us.
160 You have so many ways to cover loss!

With men, hair snatched in old age will expose
   them,
as trees lose foliage when the north wind blows
   them;
women use German pigments to conceal
grey hair: the fake tint's better than the real.
165 It isn't thick enough? What do you care?
Go blow some cash on someone else's hair.
Is buying wigs embarrassing? Oh please –
they're sold outside the shrine of Hercules.

What about clothes? Frankly, the world's too full
170 of flounces, and let's lose the purple wool.[21]
When there are many cheaper shades about,
why dress as though you took a mortgage out?
Look at the colour of the cloudless sky
when southern winds drive no rainwater by;
175 look at the colour of the golden ram
that helped the young Helle and Phrixus scram;[22]
remember sea nymphs, garbed in bluey-green
(that watercolour, called aquamarine).
Crocuses reproduce a saffron hue –
180 it's Dawn's, whose horses trail light through the dew.
Or myrtle green; amethyst's blushing face;
white roses, or the ashen cranes of Thrace;
or else the brown of chestnuts; almond brown,
or else the patina of fleecy down.
185 Numerous as flowers or spring meadows produce
when vines push grapes, and solid winter's loose,

are dyes that quench the cotton with their juice.
They won't all suit – but careful which you choose.
Grey goes with white complexions (on the day
190   when Briseis was seized, her shirt was grey)
and dark with white (Andromeda wore white:
gods scourged her island, jealous at the sight).

'Please don't have hairy legs,' I nearly wrote,
and, 'Please don't let your armpits sprout a goat.'
195   But then, my readers aren't the sort who live
in Mysia, or on some Caucasian cliff.
Why should I say, 'Black teeth are a disgrace,
and every morning, you should wash your face'?
You know to use powder if cheeks are pale:
200   art supplements the blood if blushes fail;
with art you colour in where eyebrows break,[23]
or patch up any blemish on your cheek;
it isn't wrong to put kohl on your eyes,
or saffron from Cilician crocus dyes.
205   I talked about this in an earlier book
(a smaller work, but oh, the work it took);
look up how to protect a damaged face –
I'm pleased with my research into that case.[24]

But don't let lovers see as you apply
210   what's in those boxes. Looks bloom with a lie.
Who wouldn't squirm to see you smear your cheek
with dregs that stain your bosom as they leak?
Lanolin comes from Athens, but breathe deep –

it really *is* the grease of unwashed sheep.[25]

215 Yes, use deer marrow,[26] but I can't condone
its public use. And brush teeth on your own.
It hurts the eyes, whatever joy it brings –
the finished face delights; the process mings:
the statues busy Myron made so great

220 were once hard, undressed marble, artless weight;
the silk you wear was manky wool before;
what's now a ring was once a lump of ore;
that jewel was once a stone; now it's a jade
that naked Venus' dripping tresses sprayed.

225 It's better that we think you're yet to wake up
so you can finish off fixing your make-up.
Why should I know what made your face so white?
Hide work in progress – keep the door shut tight.
Most of this stuff is gross, so never show

230 your toilet. There's so much men shouldn't know.
Gold figures gleam in theatres, so don't spoil
the illusion; they're just wood covered in foil;
when those are made, punters can take their places.
When men are absent, then put on your faces.

235 On open hair-brushing, the rule is slack.
Go on, let tangles tumble down your back.
But don't be cross if it's a bad hair day;
don't keep untying locks that slip away;
and keep your stylist safe. I'd feel alarm

240 to see you scratch her face, or prick her arm;
she'll curse the very hair that she caresses,

and weep, bleeding, about your bloody tresses.
If your hair's really bad, employ a guard,
or do it in a shrine where men are barred.
245 I was announced too quickly once, and found
a lady with her wig the wrong way round.
May such a foul faux pas befall my foes![27]
I'd rather Parthian women felt such woes.[28]
Bulls without horns are vile, fields that are bare,
250 plants without leaves, and heads without their hair.

This part's not for the truly beautiful:
Leda; Semele; Europa, tricked by a bull;
Helen, whom Menelaus, clever lad,
demanded back – whom clever Paris had;
255 ugly girls, read on – pretty ones as well
(although I find that more are *moche* than *belle*).
The loveliest don't need to master guile
because they're gifted, effortless in style:
when waters are composed, sailors can rest,
260 but squalls put their resources to the test.
Rare is a face that's free of faults; hide yours,
and, if you can, conceal your body's flaws.
If you're so short that you look seated, sit,
and work that couch. Though short, stretch over it
265 (if people size you up as you lie down,
cover your floating feet up with your gown).
If you are 'willowy', wear a thick weave;
and let it roll from shoulders in a wave;
some purple stripes will help you if you're white;

270   if black, Egyptian fish will make you bright.²⁹

Shoes made of snowy suede stop weak feet shocking;

a spindly ankle must stay in its stocking;

a bandage gives high shoulders some downsizing;³⁰

a push-up bra can keep a flat chest rising.³¹

275   When making gestures, try to keep them little

if your fingers are fat, or nails are brittle.

If you've bad breath, hush if you need to eat,³²

and if you see men, make a slight retreat,

and if your teeth are huge, or out of whack,

280   you mustn't laugh – especially if they're black.

Who would believe that girls can learn their
      laughter?

In doing so, it's tastefulness they're after.

Mouth slightly open; use your lips to hide

the tops of teeth;³³ dimples on either side.

285   You shouldn't make a long, gut-busting noise,

but some light, I don't know, feminine noise.

Some can't control their face-distorting jeers;

some laugh so hard you think that they're in tears.

Another charmless laugh's the raucous shock

290   of how a donkey brays, tied to a rock.

They even cry well. What can't skill achieve?

Whenever, however they want, they grieve.³⁴

Why do they sometimes get their letters wrong,

and, on demand, affect a stammering tongue?³⁵

295   They want to muddle words; weakness is good –

they learn to speak less ably than they should.

Consider all these things, because they work:

you have to learn to walk a woman's walk.
Deportment is the soul of etiquette:
300   it routs or rouses men you've never met.
One girl sashays with skill; her tunic flows,
catching the breeze; she proudly points her toes,
whereas an Umbrian wife, whose cheeks are red,
ambles bow-legged with a mighty tread.
305   As ever, let there be a middle way;
one is a peasant, and the other's fay.
Expose your shoulder, and one upper arm,
so someone at your side can see their charm.
This favours you, especially if you're fair.
310   I always want to kiss the part that's bare.

The Sirens were sea beasts, whose tuneful throats
were able to detain the fastest boats;
on hearing them, Odysseus nearly tugged
himself free, though his comrades' ears were
    plugged.
315   So women learn to sing. A song can bless:
more than the face, the voice is procuress.
One moment, singing show tunes is their style;
the next, they're noodling modes from near the Nile.
And women in my tutelage require
320   a quill in one hand, in one hand a lyre.
Orpheus, with his lyre, could win around
beasts, rocks, Tartarus, the three-headed hound;
Amphion sang, and rocks obeyed his call –
they dutifully formed the Theban wall.

325   And Arion was able to inspire
a mute dolphin (in legend) with his lyre.
Even learn how to sweep both hands along
Phoenician harps – they suit a jolly song.

    Study Callimachus; be keen upon
330   Philitas and drunk old Anacreon;
know Sappho (and how lewdly she behaves);
Menander's plays, with fathers conned by slaves.
Try sweet Propertius' poems; after these,
try Gallus' or Tibullus' elegies.
335   For epic, there's *The Golden Fleece*, by Varro
(for Helle, though, the ram was cause for sorrow);
or how Aeneas, prime material, came
to Rome (no Latin poem has more fame).
Perhaps my own name will belong beside
340   these greats – my writings might dodge Lethe's tide:
somebody might say, 'Read the cultured verse
he wrote to teach two sides – first his, then hers,
or the three books called *Loves*, and chose among
this oeuvre, whatever's easiest on the tongue:
345   or chant aloud *Letters of the Heroines* –
that is a whole new genre he begins.'
Please let this be the future Phoebus chooses –
please, poet soul, please, Bacchus, please, nine
        Muses![36]
Who doubts that I want girls to learn to dance,
350   and move their arms when wine gives them a
        chance?

Everyone loves stage artists when they swing –
mobility like that's a decent thing.
It's odd that I should give such small advice
as, how to rank game pieces, and throw dice.

355   Now she should throw three numbers, then mull
      over
what to call back, or craftily manoeuvre.
In 'Thieves' be cautious, yes, but not obtuse
when there are some pinned counters that you lose,
and a trapped king fights on without his queen –

360   rivals have to go back to where they've been.[37]
When balls are poured into an open net,
pick one; make sure the others aren't upset.
There is a board where lines make sections clear –
one for each month of the swift-sliding year.

365   One little board has room for rows of three –
to line your pebbles up means victory.
There are a thousand tchotchkes – it's a shame
if girls can't play them – love comes from a game.
But it's a little task to learn a rule –

370   the bigger challenge is to keep your cool.
Then we are reckless; we expose our zeal,
and our bare hearts show what we really feel.
Then in comes rage, and then a head for gain,
then rows, and fighting, and a troubling pain,

375   then accusations that resound in heaven:
each player asks the gods' help to get even.
I've often seen wet cheeks, tears freely poured
when players trust in prayer, and not the board.

Pray you be spared this ugliness – be Zen
380   if you are interested in finding men.

That's all the sport slack nature put your way;
men have more opportunities to play.
Men play with faster balls, with spears and hoops;
they kit up; they ride horses round in loops.
385   The fields of Mars, and Tiber, aren't for women –
even the virgin's cool pool you can't swim in.[38]
And yet, to Pompey's shade you should retreat
if your head's burning with the August heat,[39]
or to the Palatine, Apollo's seat,
390   recording how he sank Cleopatra's fleet,[40]
or monuments to Caesar's son-in-law,
or those built by his wife, and sister,[41] or
take trips to Isis' altars, or to plays
in three playhouses – in the public gaze –
395   or where fresh fighters' blood peppers the ground,
or see the posts that horses race around.
Don't be ignored; don't seek a hiding place –
what is the use if men can't see your face?
A secret song's pointless, though you surpass
400   Amoebeus, even blind Thamyras.
Apelles painted Venus – otherwise
she'd be submerged by waves, waiting to rise.
What does a poet want, except for fame?
We crave it – it's our labour's highest aim.
405   Once, poets were the guests of gods and kings;
the choirs that sang their work would win great things.

Sacred, majestic, worthy of the word
Prophet, they'd often reap a large reward.
Ennius earned it – from the south he rose,
410   and now his statue's next to Scipio's.[42]
Today, although we work nights for the Muses,
our ivy fades, and people call us losers.
But who'd know Homer and his tale of war
if *The Iliad* stayed in his bottom drawer?
415   And who would know Danae, if she had stayed
locked in a tower, becoming an old maid?[43]
So, pretty girls, it's wise to take your feet
over the threshold, to the crowded street.
Wolves stalk a flock with one sheep in their sights,
420   and eagles hover where birds swarm in flights.
Girls, give yourselves to crowds – be looked upon,
since, in the throng you draw, could be the one.[44]
In every place, be eager to provoke us –
it is a task demanding total focus.
425   Things happen everywhere, and it's less odd
to catch a fish if you're holding a rod.[45]
Hounds often scour the mountain glades, and yet
the stag might need no hounding to the net.
What could Andromeda, bound, hope for less
430   than that her tears find someone to impress?[46]
Some find men at men's funerals. Their feeling
flows out, their hair's a mess. This is appealing.

But do avoid the man with too much style –
who stations every hair to stand in file.

435   What he tells you, he tells a thousand girls.
        Love never stays in one place – off he whirls.
        What can you do, if he's more smooth than you,
        and probably could have your boyfriends, too?
        If Troy had shared Cassandra's understanding
440   that Paris ought to die, it would be standing.[47]
        They loiter with a phoney look of love
        and then seek to access your secret stuff.
        Don't be deceived by products in his hair,
        or by that shoe-strap, folded with such care;
445   ignore the silky toga, and the bling
        his fingers flash at you, ring after ring.
        Among such men could be a proper ponce
        who steals, and it's your wardrobe that he wants.
        Then, 'Give it back!' is what your larynx hurls
450   around the square – the cry of burgled girls.
        Venus in her gold temples, nymphs in tow,
        looks on at the injustice, but she's slow.[48]

        Some men are known for a more obvious sin:
        they stand accused of taking lovers in.
455   If someone else complains of him, believe her,
        and never be at home to a deceiver.
        Athenian girls, take care if Theseus swore,
        invoking gods that he'd invoked before.
        Sins of the father pass down to the son:
460   Phyllis lost her faith to Demophoön.[49]
        Sure, if he pledges things, your words can pledge,
        and if he gives, give him his privilege.

A woman could extinguish Vesta's flame
and pillage temples built in Isis' name,
465   and serve her man hemlock and aconite
if she takes gifts, and still denies delight.[50]

I will control myself, so Muse, hold back
the horses' reins, and keep the wheels on track.
Allow tablets on firwood to begin,
470   and have a well-trained housemaid bring them in.
Then check it: is he feigning with his art,
or is he really writing from the heart?
Write back, after a brief delay. Yes, brief:
delay goads lovers, but they need relief.
475   What does he ask? Don't swear it will be so;
but don't be obdurate when saying no.
When writing back, let him both hope and fear,
but make the cause for optimism clear.
Be stylish but straightforward when you write –
480   a conversational diction's polite.
A lover's so upset when he's in doubt,
so, beautiful, keep barbarisms out.[51]
Now, you're not married.[52] Even so, deploy
a trick that's guaranteed to fool a boy:
485   make maids or servants write instead of you,
but don't entreat those vows to someone new:
a treacherous wretch would keep the vows you
       write,
and then, as evidence, they're dynamite.
I've seen women fear that. They blanch and brood

490   while suffering perpetual servitude.[53]
       I think if someone cons you, you can con:
       if someone armed attacks, put armour on.
       That's why you need to make handwriting vary
       (perish the slaves who make it necessary!),
495   but don't reuse it until wax is scraped,
       in case the tablet holds another script.
       In letters, too, lovers should always be
       feminine, so write 'she' instead of 'he'.

       Now I should let bigger concerns prevail
500   over the small, so let me go full sail.
       Beautiful women must contain their squalls:
       calm is for humans, rage for animals.
       Faces swell, veins blacken with blood through ire:
       eyes flash more scarily than Gorgon fire.
505   Athene, when she saw it didn't suit
       her features, yelled, 'I'm giving up the flute.'
       Next time you're cross, see how your head has
          grown –
       you wouldn't recognise it as your own.
       Arrogance, too, does damage to your face –
510   love is brought on by eyes that gaze with grace.
       I hate hauteur – trust me, I've had my fill
       of silent faces flaring their ill will.
       Look back when someone looks; smile when they
          smile;
       if they make gestures, answer in their style.
515   It's only when we stop acting as brutes

that Cupid draws our spiky darts, and shoots.
I hate gloom, too. Let Ajax have Tecmessa.[54]
When glad crowds see a happy girl, they bless her.
I wouldn't want Ajax or Hector's wives.
520   I'm shocked that anyone would share their lives.
I really can't imagine you in bed,
although you must have done it, since you bred.
You mean that girls so gloomy didn't baulk
at saying 'honey', or at pillow talk?
525   Can I use great examples, without blame,
for trivial things, and use the emperor's name?[55]
Our good leader finds men whom he invites
to maintain standards, centuries and knights.
When you assess us, you, too, have to choose
530   the roles in which you think we'll be most use.
Bankers give gifts; a lawyer has his place –
he's clearly eloquent pleading a case.[56]
So let us poets do what we do best –
our chorus does love better than the rest.
535   Our job's to spread news of your grace around;
Cynthia's renowned, Nemesis is renowned;
both east and west, they've heard of Lycoris,
and many ask who my Corinna is.[57]
What's more, we visionaries travel far
540   from falsehood: art defines the way we are.[58]
Greed and ambition don't go to our heads:
we spurn the forum – worship shade and beds.
But we stick fast; love brings us to the boil;
we know too well to be loving and loyal.

545 Clearly our genius is tamed by art;
    our manners part blends with our zealous part.[59]
    A power is in them, and they are prophetic;
    the Muses like them. Girls, be sympathetic.
    God is inside us; we trade with the sky;
550 our spirit comes from palaces on high.[60]
    Don't ask a learned bard for more than song
    (alas, I've met no girl who thinks that's wrong).
    At least pretend – don't make a greedy face,
    in case it puts new lovers off the chase.

555 Horses who've only recently felt reins
    need different bridles from a horse who trains.
    Though you can catch a young man at his peak,
    for steadier souls, you need a new technique.
    A rookie, who's not known Love's tents before,
560 comes like a bull calf to your chamber door:
    make sure he clings to you, and only you;
    plant hedges round him; let nobody through.
    You'll win if it's just you. Avoid a rival –
    company threatens love's and power's survival.

565 The veteran's a wiser, slower love,
    who takes things that would make a tyro suffer:
    he won't break doors, or burn with savage blaze;
    he won't scratch nails over your gentle face;
    he won't tear up his shirt, or tear your shirt,
570 or pull your hair until you cry with hurt.
    Those things befit boys hot with youth and love;
    this fellow takes wild blows with sterner stuff.
    He burns slowly, like hay before it's dried

or timber fresh-felled from the mountainside.
575 One love is short and fruitful; one will last.
If apples go off quickly, pick them fast.[61]

I'll tell; I've given the enemy the keys.
Let's keep faith with these infidelities.
What's easy won sustains love long enough,
580 so mix your jollies with the odd rebuff.
Leave him to lie outside, to curse the door;
let him be threatening; let him implore.
Sweetness can pall: spritz us with bitter drink –
a following wind can make a vessel sink.
585 It's why a matron's love will never fizz:
she wants her husband? Oh look, there he is.
But add a door, and have some doorman rasp,
'You can't come in,' and love tightens its grasp.
Put down your dull foils – fight with sharpened steel!
590 Doubtless this is a weapon I'll soon feel.[62]
When a new lover's trapped, then he'll presume
that only he has access to your room.
Before long, let him sense he shares the honour:
without tricks of this kind, his love's a goner.
595 A thoroughbred sprints when the gate's bolts slip
with some to chase, and others to outstrip.
The deadest fires will flicker with such stoking:[63]
for me, if love's not hurting, it's not working.
Make problems vague, to keep him on his toes –
600 he'll think he has more worries than he knows.
Invent some characters: the zealous slave,

and add a husband who's a jealous knave.[64]
Sex is less vital when the coast is clear:
you might be free as Thaïs, but fake some fear.[65]

605 Although the door works fine, urge him to scurry
in through the window; let him see you worry:
make maids jump up and down and say, 'We're
  dead!',
and hide the scared youth, say, under the bed.
But keep some sex free from this kind of struggle
610 in case he doesn't want to come and snuggle.

For some reason, I was about to skip
how to give guards or smart husbands the slip.
Brides should fear husbands: keep your watch
  secure.
It's decent; right; respectful; it's the law.
615 But if the praetor's rod has set you free?
Learn from my rules how crafty you can be.[66]
To ensure co-operation, every eye
of Argos watches you, but you can lie.[67]
Write notes. You're not under a guardian's cosh
620 when you can plead time for a private wash.
Can't an accomplice take your writing far
when it can nestle warmly in her bra?
When she can hide what a deceiver writes
securely in the shoe part of her tights?
625 And if your guard is on your paper trail,
Use your aide's back – her body is the mail.
To write a message secretly, you need

fresh milk. You sprinkle carbon on to read,
and linseed oil can also help deceit:
630 its hidden message comes on a blank sheet.
Acrisius[68] guarded his daughter. Rather
than staying chaste, she made him a grandfather.
What can guards do, wherever shows take place,
when girls are keen to see a chariot race,
635 or go where men can't go, or take their rattle
to worship Isis (symbolised by cattle),
or to observe the Good Goddess's rites[69]
(the only men are those whom she invites),
or at the baths, where girls play pranks, and hide
640 while chaperones look after clothes outside,
or visiting sick friends – just well enough
to yield their beds so others can make love –
or when front doors aren't all that lovers use
(the clue is that we sometimes call keys 'loose'),[70]
645 and an excess of wine will help to banish
your guardian's wits (don't worry if it's Spanish) –
you'll find his eyelids are especially weighted
by a forgetful sleep if he's sedated –
or have a friend delay him for a while,
650 doing whatever it is that makes him smile.
But why am I prescribing all this tittle?
Bribing a guardian costs extremely little.
Nothing charms men or gods quite like a present,
and Jupiter himself finds offerings pleasant.
655 What will a wise man do, when fools love gifts?
Give him one too, and see how far he shifts.[71]

A solid, one-off bribe ought to obtain
a long while – what he gave, he'll give again.

I'm mindful of a problem that extends
660   to women as to men: beware your friends.
A dupe has pleasures she lets others pluck.
Yes, other women want to chase your buck.
You know that girl who offered us a chance
to sleep *chez elle*? I've had her more than once.
665   Don't use that maid with a too-pretty face –
if I call, and you're out, she takes your place.
What am I, mad? I'm naked in the fight –
exposed, and bringing all my faults to light.
Birds don't tell hunters where they can be found;
670   no deer gives running lessons to a hound.
Such altruism! I'll go on as planned.
Lemnian girl – my sword is in your hand.[72]
Convince us that you love us – and our trust
is won efficiently when we're in lust.
675   Watch your boy lovingly, and deeply sigh
when he arrives so late, and ask him why.
Then cry; feign grief that someone took your place,
and with your fingers, lacerate his face.
He'll have been long persuaded; he'll be sorry,
680   and say, 'Because of me, she's all a-worry.'
If he likes mirrors, and loves keeping trim,
he'll think that goddesses could worship him.
But if it hurts you, keep the damage low,
and if you hear of rivals, don't let go.

685   A quick belief can pain you: don't assume –
       learn from the tale of Procris, and her doom.

THE TALE OF PROCRIS

       There is, beside Hymettus' flowing hill
       land green with turf, and here, a sacred rill:
       there's a bright glade, and an arbutus tree,
690   and scents of laurel, myrtle, rosemary;
       thick box and fragile tamarisk align
       with slight lucerne and cultivated pine.
       There, leaves of every kind pulse on the trees,
       and grass blades tremble in the western breeze.
695   Here Cephalus finds peace upon the ground,
       having relieved his servant and his hound,
       and sings, 'Come, fluid breeze, and grant me rest;
       I'm trying to accept you in my breast.'
       His poor wife's timid ears took every word
700   because some awful zealot overheard.
       When Procris heard the name, she thought this
           Breeze
       her rival, and she suffered agonies;
       she paled, as late leaves pale lying in clusters
       of vine, hit by the strength fresh winter musters,
705   pale as the quinces, ripened, and now sweet,
       or cornelberries not yet fit to eat.
       Her mind returned, and with her nails she hurt
       her cheeks, and from her chest she ripped her shirt.
       No stopping – fury-bound, hair in a whirl,

710   she flies through streets, a raging Bacchant girl.
        She leaves her friends behind and, as she's nearing,
        strong but with silent foot, breaches the clearing.
        What did you think when, barely sane, you lay
        hid, Procris, heat burning your heart away?
715   Surely this Breeze will come, and will be caught
        in shame, with my own eyes – or so you thought.
        Now you regret it – you don't want to learn –
        now you exalt: uncertain feelings churn.
        The name, location, and the source converge –
720   she dreads what she's expecting to emerge.
        She saw the trace of where a body pressed
        in grass – her swift heart beat her shaking breast.
        Now midday shrank the shadows, then day's close
        came just as quickly; then the dawn arose:
725   there – Cephalus has come back to the place
        to splash spring water on his eager face.
        He finds his spot, while Procris hides in fear –
        he says, 'Soft breeze of Zephyrus, come here!'
        The poor girl sees the comical mistake;
730   her mind returns; her colours reawake.
        She rises; her excited body brushes
        the leaves away, and to her man she rushes:
        he thinks a beast moved. On impulse, he grasps
        the spear that even now his right hand clasps.
735   Poor boy – put down the weapon! There's no
                beast –
        no, no – the spear's in your beloved's breast.
        'Poor me,' she cries: 'you pierced a friendly heart –

this place will always suffer from your dart.
I'm dying, but not from a rival's slight,
740 and that will make the earth upon me light.[73]
On breezes I suspected, my soul flies.
I'm drifting – let your dear hand close my eyes!'
He holds her dying in his sad embrace,
and with his tears, washes the wounded place:
745 she dies, and now, the spirit, as it slips
from her incautious breast, is on his lips.

*

Back to the work. Let's lay my subject bare.
The port is near – let's steer our tired boat there.[74]
I'll take you through it now, because beginners
750 might eagerly attend my course on dinners.
Come late – drift in after they've lit the lights.[75]
Delay is good – delay leads to delights.
Drunks think you're lovely, even if you're not,
and night shades any weaknesses you've got.
755 Pick food with fingers; you should eat with grace,
so don't smear dirty paws over your face.
Don't eat before you go, and stop before
you're full.[76] Eat less than what you can – no more.
If Paris saw his Helen binge, he'd say
760 'I was a twit for taking her away.'
What's more becoming for a girl is wine –
Cupid and Bacchus go together fine.
You'll know your feet and thinking are in trouble

when your head is – the clue is, you'll see double.
765   A woman lying drunk's an ugly sight –
she'll get just anybody for the night.
And don't start sleeping when the table's clear –[77]
sleepers have many shameful things to fear.

This last part's rude, but fortunately Venus
770   said, 'We'll decide how rude it is between us.'
Observe: there's no position that will do
for everyone; find one that's right for you.[78]
So if you have a pretty face, appear
prostrate. Men like your rear? Then show your rear.
775   Milanion felt Atalantis' thighs
around his shoulders. If they're good, that's wise.
A small woman should ride. That *tour de force*
Andromache would never ride a horse.
A girl whose slinky side would turn a head
780   should flex her neck, and kneel upon the bed.
If legs are fine, and breasts a source of pride,
make the man stand, and lie upon your side.
Be like a Bacchant: liberate your locks
and let them tumble round your throat in shocks.
785   If you've been scarred in childbirth, don't display
the marks; be Parthian – ride the other way.[79]
There are a thousand postures. The least taxing
is on your right-hand side, semi-relaxing.

Horned Ammon and the tripods of Apollo
790   can't match my muse for the best tips to follow:

I've tried these things. If you trust skill, you must
trust this: my poem will repay that trust.

When she lets go, a woman ought to sense
sex in her bones, and share the experience.
795 Don't let fond voices stop, nor happy sighs;
fill up your banter with obscenities.
If nature has denied you sexual joys,
fake ecstasy with some convincing noise.
Poor woman, if that special spot lies numb
800 where happiness – hers just as his – should come.
Still, if you do fake, maintain the disguise;
be sure to move about and roll your eyes.
Panting and cries provide proof of your pleasure –
O! shameful – that part has its hidden treasure.[80]

805 And afterwards, if any women fish
for lovers' gifts, they shouldn't have their wish.
Nor should your bedroom window let in light;
some parts of you are better out of sight.

Game over: now it's time the swans depart
810 whose necks in yokes drew my poetic cart.
As men have done, women can write upon
their trophies henceforth, 'Ovid was the don.'

NOTES

[1] Penthesilea was the queen of the Amazons, a race of warrior women.

[2] A reminder that Roman poets gave public recitations to disseminate their work; even individual readers would have been chanting the verse aloud.

[3] Clytemnestra, who cheated on, and killed, Agamemnon.

[4] Eriphyle's husband Amphiarius was a prophet who knew he would die campaigning against Thebes, but she persuaded him to go anyway.

[5] Admetus had the chance to live forever, so long as he could find somebody to die in his place. His parents turned him down, but Alcestis did not. Heracles was able to rescue her from the underworld.

[6] Ovid means the physical ones.

[7] The poet avoids reminding us that these were the babies Medea killed to have her revenge on Jason.

[8] This dig at Aeneas' proverbial piety is impious in a Rome that felt itself reborn under Augustus.

[9] Stesichorus, a Greek poet, wrote that he had been blinded after he composed a disobliging poem about Helen. When he retracted it, his sight was restored. (He claimed that Helen had never been to Troy – a hint at Ovid's own seriousness here.)

[10] This passage is harsh if read as a retraction of the lines towards the end of Book 2 in praise of the older woman. They're even harsher in the context of similar sentiments in Horace, *Odes* 1.25, in which the poet mocks an ageing woman. Gibson (on ll. 69ff.) argues that 'the models draw attention to the fact that Ovid is swapping the role of teacher for that of lover'.

[11] These are examples of goddesses stooping to experience love. The moon blushes while it represents Diana, goddess of chastity. Aurora (rosy dawn) is less embarrassed by her love for Cephalus; Venus' trysts can result in children (and she doesn't age in the process, unlike the mortals Ovid warned two lines before).

[12] Ovid advances the argument that a woman suffers no physical loss from congress, and that she is as inexhaustible as the sea; and in any case, a little water clears her of the deed.

[13] This line (literally, my voice does not prostitute you) might seem odd when Augustan laws put Ovid in the position of addressing courtesans only; but it does express some diffidence about the subsequent money metaphor (literally, your gift lacks loss).

[14] The Latin word *cultus* makes a link between culture and the cultivation of one's looks. Ovid uses it to express his preference for a civilised (sophisticated) world over an innocent if crude one.

[15] As ever, it's hard to predict Ovid: will he be gallant or not? Here he again resembles Sir Walter Elliot in *Persuasion*, who sees eighty-seven women on Milsom Street, and scarcely a tolerable face among them.

[16] Ovid will give the example of the Sabine women in *Treatments* II.

[17] Ovid is as capable as other poets of aiming mockery at the modern world, as he does here; but he's not Juvenal.

[18] Pheobus = the temple to Apollo; 'lords' is a reference to Augustus' own palace.

[19] This refers to the practice of filling bays with rubble and building conspicuous villas on it.

[20] This isn't Ovid trying out a counter-argument; on this occasion, he continues to applaud care over appearance, without ostentation. As with the passage for men (*Art* 1.505ff), the advice is to avoid excess.

[21] 'Twice-dyed Tyrian purple' was à la mode in the Late Republic, and was worn as a show of wealth – it cost 1,000 denarii per pound (Gibson, ad loc.).

[22] Phrixus and his sister Helle fled from their mother Ino, when she pretended that their sacrifice would revive crops. (Helle fell off and drowned in what is now called the Hellespont.)

[23] It seems that the Frida Kahlo look was the ideal. In *Dress and the Roman Woman* (Routledge, 2008) Kelly Olson cites other sources who admire the single eyebrow. Juvenal (2.93–4) even jibes at effeminate men who try to make their eyebrows longer. Still, Olson points out, it's not a feature we find in art (pp. 62–3).

[24] Ovid is plugging *Treatments*, contained in this volume. The technical nature of this fragmented treatise bears out that he really did research. Even so, it would take more effort to prepare one of his facepacks than to write the recipe, even in Latin elegiacs.

[25] The preparation was used for inflammations or spots.

[26] Gibson cites Pliny as recommending it for ear infections, distemper and ulcers; and, cosmetically, for sores and problems with complexion.

[27] But at *Cures* 347 this could be just what you need to get over somebody.

[28] As we saw at 1.211, Parthians turn around to fire their arrows in retreat; and as we shall see at 3.786, the rear-view in love-making is the Parthian position. They are the people who do things backwards, hence the backwards wig.

[29] This reference to the 'Egyptian fish' has often been taken as a reference to crocodile dung, which is normally used as a rouge in antiquity. But Pliny recommends that you mix the dung with starch or chalk, or else starlings' droppings (Olson, pp. 61–2).

[30] Some textual uncertainty leaves commentators debating if this refers to shoulder pads, or else a bandage to push shoulders down and achieve the opposite effect.

[31] Ovid appears to be unusual among the ancients in preferring bigger breasts. The *fascia* – a bandage around the breasts – is often to make breasts look smaller: 'the ideal breast was one that a cupped hand could hold', writes Olson (p. 69). Again, though, excess would be a bad thing. In *Cures* 337–8, unbound breasts are a useful turn-off.

[32] Halitosis is less bad when the stomach has food to digest.

[33] Gibson's extensive and exemplary commentary is unusually stumped by this line. 'What exactly does this line mean?' he asks. An analogy with Marilyn Monroe might help: when she was beginning to model, she learnt to smile so that she could hide 'her excessively high gum line' (http://www.marilynmonroememories.co.uk/didyouknow.html).

[34] See note on *Cures* 690 (note 61).

[35] Lisps have always attracted people, not always decently. St Jerome

warns matrons not to allow girls to babble (*Epistle* 107.4.6, cited by Gibson); there is an analogy with Chaucer's Friar: 'Somwhat he lipsed, for his wantownesse' (General Prologue, *The Canterbury Tales*, l. 264).

[36] In this passage Ovid revisits the subject of poetry that he explored at 2.275 above. There he was chafing at the impotence of poetry in a material world; here he persuades women to learn his poetry for their own interests. Learn my stuff by heart, he argues, and you might pull. The unexpressed danger, though, is that you might pull the sort of person who writes *The Art of Love*; you could be stuck with a poet. Which, as 2.275 has told us, is not much use.

[37] Diverted but confused by discussions of Roman board games, I have envisaged something between Snakes and Ladders and chess. A modernised version of the game with the balls could be Kerplunk; the sophisticated noughts-and-crosses-style game that follows suggests that Ovid would have enjoyed playing Connect Four.

[38] This isn't so much because these places were forbidden to women; they were just very cold, and to swim in them was a mark of manliness. This is especially true of the Aqua Virgo, an aqueduct whose waters now flow into the Trevi fountain (Gibson, ad loc.).

[39] Girls are directed to the same spots as boys were in *Art* 1.67ff.

[40] Apollo was thought to have intervened in the Battle of Actium in 31 BC (when Augustus defeated Antony and gained his unrivalled authority).

[41] Buildings commemorating his wife Livia, his sister Octavia, and his son-in-law Agrippa.

[42] At least, his image appears among the worthies around Scipio's tomb. Snobbery towards southern Italy is not new.

[43] As Gibson points out, this example is a cheat. Danae was in a tower when Jupiter found her.

[44] A difficult area, this. Ovid's advice here really is aimed at prostitutes; or at least, he applies the language of prostitution to other women (if we pretend, with Ovid, that the respectable matron is not a member of his audience). It was an offence to proposition a matron in a public place. There was a loophole for the man: if the

matron wasn't dressed as a matron, but as a maid, the offence was less; if dressed meretriciously, no offence at all.

45 Literally may your hook always hang: there'll be a fish in the stream when you least expect it.

46 Andromeda, tied to a rock, had few opportunities to be seen; luckily for her, Perseus passed by.

47 Cassandra, the prophet whom Agamemnon brought home from Troy, once turned down Apollo, who gave her foresight and then decreed that no one would believe her.

48 The square is the one in which trials would take place – the Forum Iulium. There is a temple of Venus in it; her statue is not running to help.

49 As we have seen, Theseus deceived Ariadne; Demophoön was his son.

50 This is the counterpart to the advice to men at 1.449ff. There, men were encouraged to welsh on their promises, on the understanding that women are devious anyway. As in the passage on street-walking, Ovid again addresses his stated audience of sex workers: it's possible to read these lines as a ban on clipping.

51 This could be foreign phrases, or mistakes in grammar, or both.

52 Of course not. And yet, he's about to demonstrate some ruses which would surely come in handy if you were.

53 Gibson and Goold follow Damsté (1911) in placing these lines in the present order, so that ll. 489–90 precede ll. 487–8. It does make more sense if the scared women of l. 487 have something to fear.

54 'She was a captive woman, and hence melancholy,' reads the note in the Loeb edition (Mozley and Godd).

55 Ovid is comparing a woman who makes judicious use of her admirers to a chief of staff appointing officers and ministers. He does name the emperor, but indirectly, by the formal title *dux*.

56 This apparently bland line conceals a note of satire: lawyers were supposed to give their services for free, and any money they made from their work was baksheesh. (This is not unlike the days when MPs had no salaries.) Your favours, Ovid could be implying, might get you free legal advice.

[57] Cynthia is the mistress of Propertius; Nemesis of Gallus (whose poetry survives in just a few fragments); Lycoris of Tibullus. The mention of Cynthia is a paradox: we don't know her real name, so can she be famous? No and yes: we wouldn't recognise her, but the mystery generates its own éclat: who is Banksy? Who wrote *Primary Colours*? But then, do we care any longer about the real identity of the blogger who called herself Belle de Jour?

[58] The most generous understanding of this *blague* is Picasso's dictum, 'Art is a lie that tells the truth.'

[59] The word I have translated as 'genius' here is *ingenium*, which often means character. In another poem in which he talks about his decision to reject more lucrative careers (*Amores* 1.15), Ovid then goes on to celebrate his favourite poets, praising some for *ingenium* – inspiration – and some for *ars* – skill. It is a balance between luck and knack. Here, who you are makes you write the sort of poetry you write, although Ovid is not pleading for sincerity: in some ways, his poetics tally with the nineteenth-century aesthete's creed, 'The style is the man.'

[60] There are echoes here of Orphism, the belief that a divine spirit is shared among all living things.

[61] The even-handedness with which Ovid uses these couplets to play off the old and the young lover may surprise us; but it makes more sense in the context of his earlier thoughts on rough behaviour – force (*vis*) with women. To the usual tactics of hair-pulling and shirt-ripping, the young man here adds scratching; and even though these cause actual pain, as Ovid acknowledges, not even this is made to seem unwelcome. The debate is made no easier by textual problems: some texts make it seem as though the older lover is the fruitful one (reading *gravis*, severe, instead of *brevis*, short), in a line which (with another tweak) becomes, 'This love is surer, grave and more fruitful than the other.' That is the version Gibson adopts; I have gone with Mozley's Loeb text (updated by Goold in 1979). See Gibson ad loc. for a discussion of textual variations.

[62] Ovid manages to sound masochistic and ridiculous at the same time.

Like other terms to describe sexuality, it is risky to slide a modern understanding of masochism on to the ancient world (and even this construction has recently been reconstructed by some catch-all 'bdsm'). Still, for an understanding of the pleasure and pain a Roman can take from humiliation, servitude and longing, see the elegies of Propertius, whose tone is more confessional, and less self-mocking.

[63] Ovid has used this image of fire when giving the same advice to men (2.441).

[64] Naturally, this husband really would be an invention. Ovid is borrowing the stock characters of Roman comedy (which in turn are inherited from the Greek casts of Menander).

[65] Thaïs was an Athenian courtesan; but Gibson proposes that this is a reference to Menander's character of the same name, rather than the historical figure.

[66] A slave who has been freed – a freedwoman – is in a different category from a matron, and is an exemption from the law. See introduction, and Martial's ranking of options.

[67] Argos was the almost-all-seeing guard who tried to protect Io from Jupiter.

[68] He locked Danae in a tower; she had a baby with Jupiter. (See l. 415 above).

[69] The temple of the Bona Dea was for women only; she was said to blind men who came there. Still, as the next line reveals, she could easily make exceptions. Juvenal's 6th Satire, an unsparing attack on women, makes this the scene of an orgy (l. 314).

[70] In Latin, a cut key is called *adulter*. Green's translation uses the enviable pun, 'those duplicate / and duplicitous pass keys'.

[71] Some editors think this couplet spurious (Goold, for example), and it does sound like a platitude. Still, I think it's a platitude worth having, as it flatters and teases the reader at once.

[72] When the men of Lemnos took concubines, they were killed by their wives.

[73] The noblest thing Procris has to say at this point is that at least Cephalus didn't cheat on her.

74 Although Ovid's use of sailing/travelling metaphors is character-
istic of didactic poetry, there is perhaps a special purpose here. At
2.721 he uses it to represent the climax that a couple should reach
together; the echo feels all the more appropriate here as he reaches
the climactic (and raciest) part of the work.

75 This is for Delia Smith reasons – see note on 1.252.

76 Juvenal takes this further, and tackles the subject of tactical vomiting:
in his attack on women, he depicts them as throwing up to make
room for more booze (6.418–33).

77 Falling asleep is even easier at a Roman dinner party than a modern
one. Guests lie on couches, and they prop themselves up on their
elbows. Clearing the table means taking it away.

78 The lines that follow are another mark of Ovid's consistent view
that individuals should make best use of the talents they have. For
some reason, the passage on sexual positions has drawn the most
attention from scholars. Discussion continues the debate about
whom this passage is for. Is the woman pleasing the man at the
expense of her own pleasure? Is the visual nature of the writing an
invitation for men to look and fantasise, and an instruction for
women to continue obliging them? John R. Clarke (*inter alia*) thinks
so: 'Ovid is clearly providing us with the man's point of view. It is
the woman, not the man, who receives instructions on how she
should look: she must conform to the expectations of the male
gaze.'

Analogies with Roman art do something to confirm this: the
abundant nature of erotic images in Roman life, and the similarity
of frescoes to the positions described here, suggests a stronger appeal
to sight than to other senses. Still, Ovid is sparing: perhaps most of
his advice is redundant, given how easily readers could have seen
images of congress for themselves. As John R. Clarke remarks
(complains?), 'Among the "thousand ways of Venus" (*mille modi
veneris*) Ovid only comments on eight.' (p. 246).

79 A case in point: in Ovid, the position is designed to spare the man
from seeing stretch marks. Today, the comparable position called

'the reverse cowboy' is adopted with a third party, a viewer, in mind. Clarke (Plate 6) shows us a fleeting moment that was on view in the house of Caecilius Iucundus in Pompeii. A man is propping himself up on a bed from which a woman rises with her back to him. Her fingers are trailing from his fingers, or feeling for them. Across from her, at a slight distance, is an attendant. Whatever will have happened, the image is composed for a viewer, as is Ovid's *sutra*.

80 Gibson (ad loc.) observes that the poet gives women who can achieve orgasm four lines, and eight to those who can't. It leads him to agree with those who see Ovid's interest in female pleasure as an incitement to male pleasure: 'Ovid expresses sympathy . . . , but his solution is that such women should fake pleasure. This suggests that the *praeceptor*'s [instructor's] deepest concern is with the role that female pleasure plays in the male experience.' But as Gibson points out, even this advice is the counterpart to what Ovid proposes for men: see 2.307ff.

THE CURES FOR
LOVE

PREFATORY NOTE

As I remarked in the Introduction, *The Cures for Love* are a showcase for Ovid's legal training. They exist because Ovid had not yet seen through all the possibilities of mixing didactic poetry with love poetry, and also because of his instinct to see situations from their flipsides. Parts of the poem seem formulaic, especially once we have read the *Art*; we can forgive some bits of pastoral because they are parodies, but it takes a little while to see Ovid's famed psychological acuity at work.

Before long, though, we are treated to an inventory with which Freud would have been pleased. To overcome our relationship difficulties, we can try displacement activities (go farming, or hunting), sublimation (take more lovers), positive thinking (pretend you're fine) and aversion therapy – spend more time with the very person from whom you're disentangling yourself. The poem ends with a section on which food does as little as possible to stimulate love.

THE CURES FOR LOVE

1   When he read what this book is called, Amor
    said, 'I see war ahead. Prepare for war.'[1]
    'Cupid, I am your poet – please be fairer.
    How often have I been your standard-bearer?
5   Blame Diomedes! I didn't attack
    Venus at Troy, from where Mars flew her back.[2]
    I've always loved. Others are cooling off.
    But ask me what I'm doing now. I love.
    I showed how we could nurture you;[3] my law
10 brought reason where base instinct was before.
    I won't betray you, sweet boy, nor my art –
    no muse has picked my earlier work apart.
    If people love who want to love, fair play,
    and may a following wind blow them away,
15 but if they sink under a cruel girl's reign,
    then if they read this, they can live again.
    Why should a lover, unable to cope,
    swing from a roof beam, drooping in a rope?
    Why should he plunge a stiff sword in his breast?
20 Love, you love peace; but it's at your behest.
    He'll die lovesick unless he lets it halt;
    so let him, and his death won't be your fault.
    And you're a boy – all you should do is play;
    you're young, too. Yours should be a gentle sway.[4]
25 Yes, you could use bare arrows on campaign,

and yet your weapons lack a mortal stain.[5]
Spears, swords are for your step-father instead – [6]
so let him step through all the blood he's shed:
cultivate what your mother does so well –
30   don't let your errors give a parent hell.
Cause nightly brawling that makes doors fall down;
let every post be covered with a crown;
let youths and shy girls secretly connect;
let them all hoodwink husbands who suspect;
35   and let the locked out lover try to sway
and then insult the posts that won't give way.
You don't need mortal crime – enjoy the tears
and keep your torch away from funeral biers.'
I said all that, and golden Love's wings shook
40   with gems. 'All right,' he said. 'Finish your book.'

So take my lessons, disappointed youths,
whom Love took every chance to tell untruths.
Learn to be healed. I taught you love before:
the hand that brought the wound can bring the
        cure.
45   Where healthy herbs grow, poison also grows;
the nettle often stands beside the rose.
The very spear with which Achilles smote
Hercules' son became its antidote.
Not only men, but women can abide
50   by this; I'm giving arms to either side.[7]
Even if things here don't pertain to you,
examples still could show you what to do.

I recommend you snuff the flames Love gave you,
and don't let your heart's weaknesses enslave you.[8]
55 She would have lived, that poor abundant creature
Phyllis, treading nine ways, with me to teach her,[9]
and Dido, dying on the citadel,
wouldn't have seen the sails of Trojans swell;[10]
and pain would not have steeled a mum to plan
60 the bloodshed of her own, to quit a man.[11]
With my skill, Tereus would not have erred
for love of Philomel, and not turned bird.[12]
Next bring me Pasiphae; she'd leave her bull;
next Phaedra; her recovery is full.
65 Next Paris – Menelaus would still enjoy
his Helen, and there'd be no fall of Troy.
Nisus, if only your Scylla had read
my book, there'd still be purple on your head.[13]
With me in charge, men, work your feelings
through.
70 With me, let boats go straight, with all their crew.
You learnt love; you were reading Ovid then,
and now Ovid is worth reading again.[14]
I am a liberator, one who saves
the oppressed from lords, and gives freedom to
slaves.
75 Apollo, bring your laurels – I appeal
to you who taught us how to sing and heal.
Be present for the doctor and the poet:
you have the patronage of each. Bestow it.[15]
If gentle feelings give you cause for doubt –

80   if you don't like them – while you can,[16] stay out.
     When the disease is new, stamp on its seed,
     and stop the starting horse from gaining speed.
     Delay matures sweet grapes; delay brings strength
     delay makes shoots of corn attain full length.
85   The tree beneath whose broad shade ramblers sit
     was just a sapling when they planted it;
     you could have pulled it up with your bare hands,
     but look at how immeasurably it stands.
     See what you love, use a quick brain to check,
90   and if the yoke looks threatening, move your neck.
     Resist it from the start, since medicine
     is useless if a long delay sets in.
     But hurry – don't let long hours tick away –
     you'll be less fit tomorrow than today:
95   Love always lies: delay's its meat and drink –
     tomorrow you'll be free! or so you think.
     You see few rivers burst from a big source –
     with gathering streams, they multiply their force.
     Poor Myrrha never would have turned to myrrh
100 if she had quickly sensed that she would err.[17]
     I've seen wounds someone could have treated fast
     become gaping when too much time has passed.
     But we enjoy sweet Venus' fruit, then claim
     quickly, 'Tomorrow will be just the same.'
105 Still, in your guts, the silent embers creep;
     the tree of woe keeps driving roots down deep.
     So if you haven't nipped it at the start,
     and Love sits ageing in your captured heart,

it's harder. Just because you called me late,
110   it doesn't mean I'll leave you to your fate.
Heroic Philoctetes' injured limb
needed swift slicing from the rest of him,
but, after years, he managed to recover,
and thanks to him, the Trojan War was over.[18]
115   Just now I hurried to ensure your health,
and now I bring a tardy cure by stealth.
With fires, you either put them out when new,
or let them settle when their force is through:
when rage is racing, yield to rushing rage;
120   the attacking fire is tricky to engage.
The stupid swimmer doesn't know to ride
the stream obliquely, so he fights the tide.
The impatient spirit thinks himself exempt
from skill, regarding counsel with contempt,
125   but when he lets me touch the wounded spot,
and takes advice, then I can do a lot.
Who tells a mother not to mourn her son
during his funeral? It isn't done.
But when she's wept away her ailing soul
130   then words can bring her grief under control.
The knack of timing is itself a balm:
timing a draught of wine can heal or harm.[19]
A ban ignites disease, and makes it foment,
if you don't treat it at the proper moment.

135   So when you think that you can take my measure,
follow this order first: avoid all leisure.

It makes you love; it keeps that love alive;
it's food; it makes your pleasing illness thrive.[20]
Remove leisure, and Cupid's torches lie
140   flameless and scorned; his bow and arrows die.
The shady plane needs wine;[21] the poplar needs
water, and muddy soil suits marshy reeds
and Love needs leisure. Love gives way to Stuff:
keep doing Stuff, and you'll be safe enough.
145   Languor, and an uninterrupted snooze,
dicing and jiving faculties with booze
will snatch your nerves, although they never
      hurt;
then Love drifts in, if you don't stay alert.
Cupid hates doers – follows those who slack –
150   an empty head needs work to beat him back.
Go to the law, and courts;[22] flash around town
protecting friends, resplendent in your gown;
go to enjoy young men's idea of fun
in bloody war – then your delights will run.
155   The fleeing Parthians, that great new source
of pride see Caesar coming with his force:
beat Cupid's arrows, and the Parthian ones,
so you can bring two trophies home at once.
No sooner does a spear make Venus sore
160   than she demands her lover to make war.
Why did Aegisthus take another's wife?
Easy – Aegisthus had an easy life.[23]
Other men fought the lingering Trojan wars –
the whole of Greece exported every force.

165   Even if he wanted to, he never fought;
       there were no cases in his local court,
       and so he loved. How else to pass the days?
       That's how Cupid arrives, and how he stays.

       Try growing things: the country can be bliss;
170   whatever cares you have give way to this.[24]
       Yoke up some tame bulls' necks,[25] and make them
          toil,
       so that the ploughshare wounds the hardy soil;
       bury some grains in cultivated earth
       so that the land returns more than it's worth.
175   See branches sag from apples plump with juice
       till trees hardly sustain what they produce;
       how streams gurgle with chuckles as they pass,
       and watch your flock chomp down the fertile grass.
       See how the goats find rocks and craggy crests,
180   then come back to their kids with sagging breasts;
       on pan pipes, shepherds improvise a song
       accompanied by dogs in busy throng;
       elsewhere deep forests resonate with moos
       as mothers chase the calves they'd hate to lose.
185   Then there are swarms to smoke out their homes
       and hives that need relieving of their combs.
       Autumn gives apples; summer's harvest's gold;
       spring offers blooms; fire tempers winter's cold.
       At the right time the farmer plucks the fruit
190   of vines, squeezing its juice with naked foot;
       at the right time he has hay bales to make,

and steady soil to comb with a fine rake.
Here you have gentler water brooks to lead
to field where you can plant the shooting seed.
195 The grafting time is here: a branch receives
another branch, and grows with alien leaves.
The moment minds are mulched by all these things,
Love drifts off on debilitated wings.

Or else go hunting: Venus yields her place
200 when Phoebus' chaste sister gives her chase.
So let the wily pups loose on the hare,
and find a leafy ridge to stretch your snare,
or with a start disturb the nervous deer,
or make the boar fall to a head-on spear.
205 At night, no girl-care takes your wearied breast –
it's sleep that makes your limbs heavy, with rest.
A gentler passion (but the sort one needs)
is chasing little birds with nets or reeds,
or else hiding a metal hook with treats
210 the greedy-mouthed, misguided fishy eats.

Then, one way or another, you can con
yourself, till all knowledge of love is gone;
and so, although the chains of love are strong,
you will go far, and may your route be long.
215 You'll weep; your lover's name is coming back;
your footstep will be often stuck mid-track.
The less you want to go, the more you must –
let your reluctant feet kick up the dust.

Don't let rains or the Sabbath make you stay,
220 nor the remembered dead of Allia day.[26]
Don't count miles that you've gone, miles yet to
    roam,
nor make excuses to be close to home.
Be like the Parthians: don't keep looking back
at Rome. Parthians retreat when they attack.

225 Some say that my instructions are a strain
but, to be strong, you have to bear the pain.
Though I've complained, I've been without a meal
or drained a bitter draught when I've been ill.
To cure your body, you'll take fire and steel
230 and shun water, however parched you feel.
What won't you tolerate, then, for your mind?
That organ's value leaves the rest behind.
The opening's by far the hardest part –
the biggest task before you is the start.
235 You know how yokes give captured bulls a rash,
and new bits hurt swift horses when they dash?
Maybe to leave the home and land you know
will sadden you. You'll look back, but you'll go:
it isn't home or land, but the old flame
240 that calls you back. Fine words cover your shame.
But once you're off, friends and the countryside
and travel make a hundred worries slide.
Go for a while – it's not enough to dash –
wait for the flame to wither into ash.
245 If you return without a settled mind,

Love strikes with all the weapons he can find.
You'll come back hungry, thirsty from the road,
and feel the worse for the whole episode.

Do you believe dark arts can bring relief?
250 You trust Haemonian herbs? Test that belief.
Old poison lies that way. Apollo's cure
comes from his sacred song, and is more sure.[27]
I won't make spirits leave the tombs they haunt;
no crones will cleave the earth or grimly chant;
255 no field will give another field its wheat
nor will the sun suddenly lose its heat.
The Tiber's waters flow the way they flow;
the moon's still drawn by horses white with snow.[28]
There is no heart that chanted passion off,
260 and burning sulphur doesn't banish love.
How could all Colchis' home-grown grass relieve
Medea when she didn't want to leave?
Circe, what use were all your mother's plants
when fair winds blew away the Ithacans?
265 You tried to keep your guest, to no avail:
the trickster saw his chance, and went full sail.
You tried to keep your heart from heavy burning –
in your unwilling heart, Love still sits, turning –
you, who could turn men into any shape.
270 But from your own heart, there was no escape.
Still, when Odysseus wanted to go,
then you addressed him, trying to keep him, so:
'Odysseus, I will not now implore

to be your wife, although I did before
275 (and yet I'm more than fit to be your wife –
I am a goddess – Phoebus gave me life).
Don't rush, I beg – the biggest thing that I'm
praying for, as a gift, is simply time.
The water's choppy; that should worry you.
280 You want a later wind to see you through.
Why should you flee? No new Troy's on the way;[29]
no one asks you to fight another day.
Here, there is peace, and love, which hurts just me.
Your kingdom will be safe, so let it be.'[30]
285 She spoke. Odysseus pushed his boat towards
the sea. Winds and his sails took useless words.
Circe tried all her usual tricks, and raged.
It's not the way that passion is assuaged.
So if you're after my advice, ignore
290 poisons and chanting spells. They aren't a cure.

But if some mighty cause keeps you in town,
I have advice for you, so take this down:
a liberator's heart bursts from its thrall
if he is free from pain once and for all.
295 I'd be amazed, though, and I'd say to you,
'You don't need me to tell you what to do.
You want to go, but can't? You should be turning
to me if you've a problem with unlearning.
Remind yourself of what your girl has done,
300 and summon up her misdeeds, one by one.
She took so much, but that wasn't enough –

the greedy girl has sold my townhouse off.
She promised, but was lying when she swore.
How many times I lay outside her door!
305   But she loves others now; spurns my affection;
the salesman gets her, and I get rejection.'
Let these thoughts totally contaminate
your senses; keep them; seek the seeds of hate.
You wish you could be witty when you're crying?
310   So cry, and wit will come without you trying.
Just recently, I carried a firm flame
for somebody who didn't feel the same.
I thought I'd treat myself with my own trick,
but I admit, then I got really sick.
315   So then I kept remembering her faults,
and that revived me like a dose of salts.
'How dreadful are her legs!' I used to sigh,
although I must confess that was a lie.
'Her arms are rather less than lovely, too,'
320   although I must confess that wasn't true.
'She's too short (no she's not); she asks too much –'
Ah – that gave my disdain its surest touch.
Good things and bad are often side by side –
we err, so sometimes virtues are denied.
325   Where possible, rethink your girlfriend's gift –
hoodwink your judgement with a tiny shift.
So dusky girls are black; 'curvy' is rated
as fat, and thin girls are emaciated.[31]
If she's not simple enough, then call her rude;
330   if she's too simple, then call her a prude.

And even think of things that she can't do.
Tell her she can – she'll do them just for you.
Urge her to sing, if her voice isn't sweet,
and make her dance if she has two left feet.

335 Her speech is crude? Then that's what you require.
She didn't learn to play? Get her a lyre.
She'll walk that heavy walk. Her bosoms fall
about her chest? She needs no bra at all.
She has bad teeth? Then tell her something funny,

340 or something sad to make weak eyes go runny.
And, if your girlfriend isn't done adorning
herself, go see her first thing in the morning.
We fall for make-up, and accessories
hide much – they're most of what a woman is.

345 Amid all this, you'll look for what you love –
abundant Amor traps you with this stuff.
Come unannounced – she's unarmed in the wars –
the luckless woman falls because of flaws.
Sometimes it's not worth trusting this advice:

350 beauty can trick you without artifice.[32]
So when she slathers dyes upon her face,
don't be embarrassed – go round to her place.
You'll see boxes of stuff of every hue,
and breasts dripped on by grease of unwashed ewe.[33]

355 These treatments reek of what Phineus eats –
it makes my stomach heave, and it repeats.[34]

Because all love needs knocking on the head,
let me explain how you should be in bed.

To say too much about this is demeaning,
360 but if you're smart, you'll catch most of my
     meaning.
The Of late my readers cavil, and accuse
my work of having a disgraceful Muse.
So long as my work pleases, and is famous,
what does it matter if some people blame us?
365 Envy made Zoilus knock at Homer's fame.[35]
But without Homer, who'd know Zoilus' name?
And there are sacrilegious tongues that smear
the tale of how the Trojan gods came here.[36]
Supreme achievement is what envy seeks,
370 as winds sweep heights, and lightning bolts blast
     peaks.
Whoever you are, whom my freedom offends,
see sense – your rhythm should reflect your ends.[37]
Tough wars fit neatly into Homer's meter,
but is it quite the beat for something sweeter?
375 Tragedians sound grand – wear tragic boots;
for ordinary scenes, the *soccus* suits.[38]
The iamb's what you use against a foe,
whether you make it swift or limping slow.[39]
Let Elegy be friendlier, and hymn
380 cupids, and caper nimbly at her whim.[40]
Homer can't do Callimachus; meanwhile
Achilles bucks Callimachean style.
You can't cast Thais as Andromache,
and the reverse, too, is a liberty.
385 But Thaïs suits my art – it's wanton, free,

136

and not for matrons. Thaïs is for me.
And if my muse responds to jolly themes,
we've won – she's not as guilty as she seems.
Eat till you pop, Envy: I'll have great fame –
390   still greater, if my progress stays the same.
Envy, you're hasty – while I live, you'll fret –
my wit has many songs to capture yet.
My love of fame grows with renown, and thrills:
my horse pants at the foot of lower hills.
395   I do for Elegy what Virgil did
for Epic when he wrote the *Aeneid*.

You've answered Envy, poet. Now pull back
the reins; continue in your proper track.
So when there's sex, and youthful labour planned,
400   and when the long-awaited night's at hand,
for fear your girlfriend captures you, make sure
you've had sex with another, just before:[41]
find somebody who'll quickly satisfy you,
so come the next time, earlier feats defy you.
405   Love held back pleases most; when cold, we crave
the sun; in sun, a shower, in thirst, a wave.
Should I say this? I will – when joining her,
adopt positions that you least prefer.
It's not hard – girls have faults, but don't admit
    them –
410   there's no position they think doesn't fit them.
If your windows have shutters, take them off –
looking at limbs in noonday sun is rough.[42]

But when you've reached the finish line, and come
(when flesh retires, and when your sense is dumb),
415   you wish you hadn't touched her, and you'd rather
a while goes by before you touch another,
check where all her physical weakness lies,
and hold her faults up to your inner eyes.
If some would call a flaw a tiny spot,
420   and one won't do the trick, then spot a lot.
Small vipers topple oxen with a bite,
and dogs detain a boar in all its might.
Have numbers on your side: you should collate
all my advice; the pile-up will be great.
425   But since love happens in so many ways,
my lessons don't apply to every case.
What mightn't seem a crime to everyone
is crime by somebody's criterion.
One lover's love stops almost as it starts
430   because he sees his girlfriend's private parts;
one rallied when his girl rose to her feet
and left post-coital schmutzes on the sheet.
These trifles make a trivial lover turn,
and feeble torches make his passion burn;
435   but Cupid bends his bow to hurt you more –
the injured parties need a stronger cure.
What of the man who stalked a girl, and hid
while she excreted, though customs forbid?
Dear gods, I won't ask that of anyone.
440   It might well work, but simply isn't done.
Rather, I recommend that you take two

girlfriends, or even better, take a few.
Brains flit between two options when they split:
first love yields to the love that follows it.
445   Channelling makes a mighty river small:
spreading out logs will make a high flame fall.
One anchor's not enough to hold a ship –
in running depths, a single hook will slip:
the old hero who had troubles to tell
450   two lovers triumphed in the citadel,
whereas today, if you have wrongly reckoned
that one girl's worth it, go and find a second.
Procris made Minos' first wife[43] the lesser;
also, Idaea trumped her predecessor.[44]
455   To keep Alphesiboea from his head
Alcmaeon took Callirhoe to bed.
Paris would suffer till the end of days
had Helen not taken Oenene's place.
Tereus' wife was lovely; he'd resist her
460   only because of her imprisoned sister.[45]
The list's tiring. Won't these examples do?
Every love's beaten by somebody new.[46]
A mother is less sad to lose a son
if she has more; sadder if there's just one.
465   In case you think I'm laying down new laws
(if I'd thought this up, think of the applause!),
when Agamemnon saw (because he sees
all things, because he is the king of Greece)
the captive Chryseis, he fell in love.
470   Her father wept. What was he thinking of?

Stupid, hateful old man. They are both fine;
you're damaging your daughter when you whine.
So when Calchas[47] had issued the command
that she should be restored to her own land,

475   the king said, 'One girl's beauty is the same –
one syllable aside, so is the name,[48]
whom smart Achilles willingly will yield –
but if he won't, he'll know what power I wield.
If any of you Greeks think this is wrong,

480   the hand that holds the sceptre's very strong.
If I'm a king without a concubine,
then even Thersites can have what's mine.'[49]
This consolation for his first despair
meant care gave way to a new kind of care.

485   So be like Agamemnon – feel a surge;
leave your old lover where your paths diverge.
Where will you find them? Go back through your
      notes.
There are enough for you to fill whole boats.[50]

Now, if I have something of use to teach

490   (or if Apollo lectures through my speech) –
if Etna's core is burning you, poor fool,
then make your face assume a glacial cool:
although you grieve, look healthy, to beguile
suspicious girls; and though you're weeping, smile.

495   I'm not suggesting you dry up, mid-care –
the orders of my rule aren't so unfair.
Seem what you're not: pretend your rage is ended,

and soon you'll be the way that you intended.
To dodge a drink, I look like I'm asleep;
500 I shut my eyes, and then love comes on deep.
I once saw someone simulating love,
who fell in his own trap. That made me laugh.
It takes practice to learn love, and unlearn:
pretend you're healthy; then health will return.
505 She asks you round. You go, as promised, but
be patient when the door's already shut.
Don't try to chat up or insult the door,
nor run at it until your sides are sore.
Then day will break. Don't let your words
   complain:
510 your face should show no vestige of your pain.
She'll be less haughty when she sees you're fine
(fringe benefits come from this art of mine).[51]
But fool yourself, too – don't think love will end –
that thought's like reins with which horses contend.
515 Do what is fruitless – let yourself forget
it's useful. Birds avoid too big a net.
Don't let her be too happy, or too cross,
and if you argue, make her feel the loss.
If she calls out to you, walk past her door,
520 and if she names a night, say you're not sure.
You'll miss the date, but bear the loss with ease.
Just go and find some other easy squeeze.

Now who could call my method hard too endure?
Look, I'm a marriage guidance counsellor.

525 Since natures vary, we vary our skills –
a thousand treatments cure a thousand ills.
The malady that no excision curbs
might well give way to medicines and herbs.
Are you a softy? Bound up? Held in check?
530 Does Cupid have his foot upon your neck?[52]
Don't struggle – go wherever typhoons blow,
even if it's back home. Row with the flow.
Yes, quench the thirst that nearly left you dead –
I'll let you drink straight from the fountain head –
535 then, overquench your thirst. Don't merely dull it –
let water's superabundance drench your gullet.
Enjoy your girlfriend – no one's in the way:
let her divert you every night and day.
Aim to be bored – boredom will bring the end.
540 You think you'll go without, but then you'll spend
the night, then horde the love that you're enjoying –
and then love goes. Her company is cloying.

Anxiety can make love last for years.
You want to banish love? Then banish fears.
545 If you dread rivals, and that she'll move on,
you're almost past the skill of Machaon.[53]
A mother of two sons will love one more
if she's afraid he won't return from war.
Beside the Colline Gate, there is a shrine
550 named after Eryx, born of Venus' line.
There Love makes you forget your suffering,
dousing his torches with an icy spring.

There youths ask to be free of vows again,
and trapped girls to be free of stubborn men.
555   Love said (was it Love, really? He did seem
like Love; more likely, though, it was a dream):
'Ovid, you teach love, then take it away?
There's something else your manual ought to say.
Think of your problems. Love will then be gone.
560   God gives woes (more or less) to everyone.
Some dread the stock exchange, and are upset
on dates when they repay a rising debt;
if your father's a bastard, though you've got
all that you wanted, look at him a lot.
565   The poor man with the poorly dowried wife
can think she's why he's ruining his life.
You have big fields, good country to produce
your vines? Worry they won't have any juice.
You have a cargo coming? Then abjure
570   the cruel sea – your goods are on the shore.
Your daughter's eligible, your son's a warrior –
there are a thousand reasons to be sorrier.
Paris could put his girl out of his head
by looking at his slain brothers instead.'
575   He went on more, and then his boyish gleam
fled from my dream (if it was just a dream).
In midsea, Palinurus left his ship.
What can I do? This is an unplanned trip.[54]

For lovers, lonely places aren't allowed.
580   Don't go there. You're much safer in a crowd.

Secrets are no use; secrets stoke your longing.
You're better off wherever folk are thronging.
If you're alone, the face of her you left
hovers before your eyes, and you're bereft.
585   That's why the night is sadder than the day:
the troop of friends – your allies – is away.
Be chatty; let your chums visit your place;
don't let the shadows hide your sorry face.
Be like Orestes – have a Pylades,
590   who'll always firmly share your sympathies.[55]
And what was it that brought on Phyllis' end?
Not just the secret woods – she had no friend.
She rushed about, hair tumbling down her back
like Bacchant crowds at their triennial craic.
595   She looked as far out as she could, and scanned
the sea, then slumped exhausted on the sand.
'Demophoön, you bastard,' she would screech,
and sudden sobs would interrupt her speech.
There was a narrow pathway that the trees
600   shadowed, and this would lead her to the seas.
She walked the path nine times, and said, 'He'll see!'
She blanched – looked at her belt, and then a tree.
She hesitates – fear comes on her, to check
her daring – she puts fingers round her neck.
605   I wish you hadn't been alone. The leaves
fall from the branches – all the forest grieves.
So learn from this – don't scurry to your den,
you men wounded by girls, girls hurt by men.

One man took my advice, and followed it,
610   so I discharged him as completely fit,
but then he lapsed. On Lover's Lane he'd stray –
Cupid took up the darts he'd put away.
If you're in love, but wish you weren't, avoid
contagion: that way livestock is destroyed.
615   You see the sufferers; after the inspection
you suffer too. Much harm comes from infection.
Water will sometimes trickle from nearby
into an area where soil is dry:
love trickles under cover if you stay[56]
620   (and that's a game that all of us can play).
Another man was cured, then couldn't stand
seeing his girl – she hurt by being at hand.
The wound reopened where the scar had lurked
and none of my love-curing craft had worked.
625   A blaze blown from next door is hard to quell –
if you can leave the quarter, you'll do well.
Don't cultivate her friends. The colonnade
that shelters her should never give you shade.
The fire is out – why let reminders fan it?
630   If possible, go to another planet.
What hungry man holds back from the buffet?
Who isn't thirsty where spring waters play?
When stallions see mares, they neigh forever;
no bull's restrained when he beholds his heifer.
635   You've nearly reached the shore, but bear in mind
she's not the only one to leave behind:
there's still her sister, mother, knowing nurse,

and all remote associates of hers.
The slave comes, or a maid pretends to cry,
640   guilt-tripping you: 'My mistress just says hi.'
You'd ask, 'What is she up to?' but be strong:
your only profit is a tangled tongue.
And those of you who could a tale unfurl,
and carry on complaining of your girl –
645   stop it. That way, her memory will take flight,
and anyway, your silence serves her right.
Silence beats claiming that you've had enough.
Telling the world you're not in love proves love.
Better to put a fire out bit by bit
650   than quickly. Stop slow. You'll get over it.
A torrent might be deeper, and go fast.
It's brief, though. An unbroken stream will last.
Let love fail, evanescent on the breeze,
and let passions expire by slow degrees.
655   But hating those you've loved is criminal:
that kind of end befits an animal.
Not caring's fine, but ending love with hate
keeps love, or keeps you in a sorry state.[57]
It's ugly when a couple starts to fight –
660   Venus herself would never think it right.
Men often love the women they accuse –
where there's no quarrel, there's no love to lose.
I once advised a man who saw the litter
belonging to his wife.[58] His threats were bitter.
665   He could have left. He hollered, 'Out you come!'
So out she came. He saw her, and was dumb.

He dropped the list of everything she'd done;[59]
he held her in his arms and said, 'You've won.'
Depart in peace: that path's proper, less fraught
670　than those that lead from courtship to the court.
Let her keep what you gave without a fuss –
you'll have greater advantage, and less loss.
But if, by some unhappy chance, you meet her,
deploy the tactics that I taught to beat her.
675　Man up; chase weapons: fight her from the start –
conquer Penthesilea with your dart.
Remember rivals, and the nights you stayed
on her harsh doorstep, and how much you prayed.
If you're about to meet, don't brush your hair,
680　or wear your toga's folds as if you care.
Don't make an effort – after all, she's gone.
There are so many girls, and she's just one.[60]

What is the worst impediment of all?
We've all had some experience to recall.
685　We hope we're loved – we're slow to walk away –
we're vain – we fall for everything they say.
Ignore those voices (what could be less true?):
don't think of what the eternal gods can do.
Don't be convinced, either, by women's tears –
690　they've been training their eyes for many years.[61]
Many techniques sap spirits from a lover,
as rocks erode that gentle waters cover.
Never reveal your reasons for the split.
Don't share your pain. Rather, hold on to it.

695   Don't bring up charges she can mitigate
       in case her counter-charges hold more weight.
       Don't preach of anything that she did wrong,
       or she'll reply. The silent man is strong.
       I'd not steal arrows, like Odysseus might,[62]
700   or filch Love's torches, to put out his light,
       nor would I try to clip his purple wing,
       nor would my teaching slacken his bow's string.
       Obey the song; I sing what I advise –
       healthy Apollo, bless this enterprise.
705   Apollo's here, and all the signs are clear –
       the lyre – the quiver – yes, Apollo's here.
       Amyclaean wool, dyed in big tubs of brass
       is rubbish. Purple from Tyre's a different class.
       Compare your girl to those the world adores,
710   and soon enough, you won't think much of yours.
       Goddesses look divine, but Venus won
       when Paris had to make comparison.
       Compare manners and skills, not just the face,
       and in deciding, don't give love a place.

715   Next, I have just a tiny thing to tell,
       but it's helped many people (me as well):
       avoid re-reading letters that you've kept –
       some hardy spirits have re-read, and wept.
       Gather your billets-doux, and burn them all,
720   saying, 'This is my ardour's funeral.'
       Althaea burnt a log, and hence her boy,[63]
       so burn those lying letters. Why be coy?

Remove all waxworks, too. What can be gained
from wax? That's how Laodamia waned.[64]
725 Places are damaging, and so refrain
from visiting old love nests: they cause pain.
'Yes, she was here – she lay here; and I treasure
the room in which she gave me lusty pleasure.'
A memory chafes Love; the old wound tears –
730 the weak quickly succumb to feeble cares.
If you add sulphur to the cooling ash,
then embers flare up in a mighty flash;
so, if you don't avoid what sparks Amor,
the flame flickers where there was none before.
735 Greek sailors must regret they hit the reef
where an old man's false lights avenged his grief.[65]
The cautious helmsman's happy to avoid
Scylla: beware the spots that you've enjoyed.
Steer past the craggy rocks, the sands, and dodge
740 dreadful Charybdis as she vomits sludge.

Sometimes, things that you can't control by force
go so much better when fate takes its course.
Poseidon's bull would never rise to dash
Hippolytus if Phaedra had no cash.[66]
745 Had Pasiphae been poor, she'd have seen sense;
indulgent love survives on opulence.
Nobody took kind old Hecale or
Irus the beggar – they were both too poor.[67]
Poverty has no means to feed romance.
750 (That doesn't mean it's worth taking the chance.)[68]

Nor is it worthwhile taking in a show
while hearts are waiting for their love to go.
The spirit stirs with flutes, zithers and sweet
singing, and lyres, and dancing to the beat.

755 The choreography tells lovers' stories;
acts show how pleasing what you should abjure is.
With heavy heart, I say, you should eschew
the gentler poets – my own offerings, too.[69]
Avoid Callimachus: he's not love's foe.

760 For the same reason, Philitas must go.
Sappho once made me better to my love;
Anacreon's precepts aren't remotely tough.[70]
Who safely opens up Tibullus' cover
or reads the poetry of Cynthia's lover?

765 Who turns from Gallus with a hardened heart?
My own work has a similar sort of art.

Unless Apollo has deceived his bard,
rivals make your recovery really hard.
Don't picture other people in her bed:

770 imagine that she's all alone instead.
Orestes fell under Hermione's spells
much more when she took up with someone else.
Stop moaning, Menelaus. You didn't take
your wife to Crete. You gave her quite a break.

775 Then Paris took her, then you couldn't go
without; another's love made your love grow.
Achilles wept when Briseis had gone
to experience the joys of Atreus' son.

He wept with reason. You'd be quite a slob
780 not to have taken that perk of the job
(I'm not so smart, but I'd have done the same)
and from that fruit, a mighty quarrel came.
She was untouched, the king swore, by his rod
of office; but a sceptre's not a god.
785 Let gods help you walk down your ex's street
and pass her door with fit-for-purpose feet.
It's possible – you have to hold your course,
and dig a spur into your speedy horse.
Pretend that there are Sirens on the shores,
790 and Lotus eaters; hasten sails with oars.
As for the rival who once made you sore –
don't cast him as the villain any more,
but say hello, although you might be bitter,
and when you can embrace him, you'll be better.

795 Now, food. I'm sitting in the doctor's seat
to tell you what you should and shouldn't eat.
No matter where good onions can be had –
Libya, Megara, here – they're all as bad.
Avoid rocket as much; or any stuff
800 that helps you limber up your limbs for love.
Rue is more salutary – it denies
your limbs that love – it's so good for the eyes.[71]
You ask what do I think of Bacchus' gift?
You won't be waiting long to catch my drift.
805 The vine prepares a soul for Venus, but
the heart drowns if there's lots, and it's uncut.

A wind can nourish or put out a fire,
feeds it if low, and kills it if it's higher.[72]
Either don't drink, or drink enough to clean
810   your cares away – the worst is in between.[73]

I've finished – now my vessel's prow can sport
a garland as I sail into the port.
Before long, men and women will applaud
the poetry by which they are restored.

NOTES

1 The opening of *Cures* echoes that of the *Amores*; there, Ovid was planning to write an epic about war, when Love interrupted and took a metrical foot away from the verse, so that the genre switched to erotic elegy. Ovid wins this rematch.

2 *Iliad* 5.330

3 In the *Art*.

4 At the beginning of the *Art* the poet drew attention to the paradox that someone so small should be so powerful. Here, he urges the boy to use less power: the *Art* has established it, and now it needs dismantling.

5 Having argued that love can lead to death, Ovid asks, does it have to be that way?

6 Mars, god of war, is called this (with a Latin pun) because of his role as Venus' beau.

7 Ovid has argued this already in the section of the *Art* devoted to women; now he's reasserting the parity of his advice, but what follows makes this sound unlikely.

8 What could be simpler? It sounds like the Duke of Wellington's advice to a young officer with romantic troubles: 'You are in a dashed difficult situation. You must do your best to get out of it.'

9 Ovid gives us the aetiology of this epithet at l. 591ff. below.

10 Dido, Queen of Carthage, was Aeneas' host. When he left her to found Rome, she stabbed herself on top of her funeral pyre. It is the subject of Virgil's *Aeneid*, Book 4.

11 Medea would not have taken Jason's desertion so hard.

12 Tereus became a hoopoe, having raped Philomela and silenced her by cutting out her tongue. Philomela became a nightingale (as Ovid tells it in *Metamorphoses* 6 – in Greek myth a swallow). In introducing his *Tales from Ovid*, Ted Hughes reminds us of the influence of this tale on *Titus Andronicus*.

13 For Pasiphae, see *Art* 1.289ff. Euripides' *Hippolytus* tells of how Phaedra fell in love with her stepson. Nisus had purple hair, which

his daughter Scylla cut off to give to her lover, Minos. See *Art* 1.331, and note.

[14] It is impossible not to hear the master phrasemaker writing his own blurb here.

[15] Now that Ovid sets himself up as a doctor, his language becomes more medical, and his imperatives read like prescriptions.

[16] The wording here is identical to that at *Art* 1.41, when the poet is offering advice on the start of the affair. There, the 'while you can' entertains the possibility that you might still have a choice about whether or not you fall in love. Ironically, the ideal reader of *Cures* is assumed to be in just the same situation. It reminds us that *Art* can be just as cynical about love – one-on-one, exclusive love – as *Cures* is.

[17] See *Art* 1.288 and note.

[18] When the Greek warrior Philoctetes hurt his foot, it smelt so noisome and gangrenous that his comrades left him on Lemnos. But when it was foretold that the Trojan War would only end with Philoctetes' magic bow, the Greeks did their best to placate him. He finally agreed, and was restored.

[19] Wine was used as medicine in ancient times.

[20] The idea that love can be bittersweet goes back at least as far as Sappho, who devised the term (*glukupikron*). For her acute, physical treatment of love as a kind of ailment, she too was considered a physician.

[21] The tree was supposed to benefit from the wine people poured for it as a libation when they were drinking under its shade.

[22] One of the better jokes in the *Cures* is to hear Ovid adopt the voice of the competitive man who follows the Roman 'course of honours' (*cursus honorum*). This is what he attacks with some bitterness at *Amores* 1.15, when he is defending his own position in society as a poet.

[23] Aegisthus was the man who took Agamemnon's place in Clytemnestra's bed when the latter was away at Troy. Ovid's view chimes with that of the chorus in Aeschylus' *Agamemnon*, who call

Aegisthus a wolf lying in a lion's lair (l.1224).

24 The following passage may have the occasional touch of banality, but there are at least two layers of parody going on: the practical information about farming recalls Virgil's *Georgics*, a didactic poem about how hard farming is if you're going to do it properly; and the suggestion that the countryside is idyllic echoes Virgil's earlier *Eclogues* (which in turn take Theocritus' *Idylls* as their model). The problem is that the *Eclogues* do portray forlorn and frustrated lovers, particularly the second one. It is hard not to conclude that Ovid is exploiting this contradiction to add another layer of parody – a mockery of himself, the urban sophisticate who thinks that agricultural work will be diverting.

25 Note how often this is used as an image to subdue lovers, or to submit to love. Here it is literal, but all the more fake for the metaphorical versions that have preceded it.

26 See note on *Art* 1.413.

27 I.e., trust this poem.

28 Ovid's dislike of magic leads him to the *adunaton* – the expression of the impossible. But whereas other poets will use it to name the impossible things that are possible to, say, a singer such as Orpheus, here the earthier Ovid uses it to say: no, really, no matter what you do, the following things can't happen.

29 While Odysseus is with Circe, Aeneas is leaving Dido to found the second Troy that will become Rome. There is a hint from Ovid that Circe is so gifted with prophecy that she can see the *Aeneid* coming.

30 She's right about this, too, but given the state that Ithaca's in without Odysseus, it sounds like a lie for now.

31 Many tricks from *Cures* turn out to be inverted tricks from *Art*. This one comes from 2.661.

32 A book of photographs by Véronique Vial, *Women before 10 a.m.*, illustrates this point.

33 Lanolin.

34 Phineus was cruel to his sons, and so the Harpies made his food reek.

35 Zoilus was a critic, and was harsh about Homer (3rd century BC).

36 Not even Virgil's *Aeneid* is free from detractors.

37 Ovid is arguing that if he is going to offer more intimate advice on how to become disenchanted, at least he's doing it in the right genre. (A consequence of this is that it's our fault if we didn't notice the elegiac couplets and prepare ourselves for scenes of a sexual nature from the start.)

38 The cothurnus – the tall buskin – was the footwear for tragic actors; the soccus of comic actors was shorter. Again, a nod towards theatre allows Ovid to point out that he isn't breaking new ground.

39 Some of Catullus' rudest poems are in this metre.

40 Ovid personifies his metre.

41 Ovid's apparent awkwardness about offering this tip might have something to do with the importance he places on shared and simultaneous pleasure at various stages in the *Art*. Is his concern, not that it's obscene, but mean? It's more likely in modern times to hear a similar (easier) technique prescribed, but in the interest of making the subsequent date more of a success. This ploy is more pragmatic than tantric: 'if you're smart [or have seen *There's Something about Mary*] you'll catch my meaning.'

42 In *Amores* 1.5, a suggestive recollection of a sexual encounter, Ovid tells us quickly, first, that it's a hot afternoon, and then that the shutter is closed.

43 Pasiphae.

44 Her predecessor as Phineus' wife was called Cleopatra.

45 He preferred Philomela to Procne.

46 Louis XV's doctor told him that the greatest aphrodisiac is change.

47 Calchas was the high priest to the Greek forces; a prophecy told him that the army's plague would not abate unless Chryseis was restored to her father (*Iliad* 1).

48 The name of Briseis even sounds like that of Chryseis.

49 Thersites was a lowly discontent among the Greeks. Odysseus beat him up to roars of approval.

50 As with the advice on delaying tactics at ll. 403–4 above, Ovid comes

perilously close to handing out tips that an actual lover might find handy. Here he refers us back to the *Art*, Book I.

51 Is this another occasion when, in spite of the poem, Ovid repays his debt to pleasure?

52 This is the trope that represents love's servitude (the *servitium amoris*). It symbolises the relationship between the conqueror and the conquered. Propertius opens his oeuvre with it.

53 A Greek doctor at Troy.

54 The link from the dream to Palinurus is artful. Palinurus is the helmsman in the *Aeneid* who is overcome by sleep, and falls to his death from the ship. Ovid's own narrative is similarly ambushed by a divine agency. He suggests that his digressions aren't his fault.

55 The friendship between Orestes, son of Agamemnon and Clytemnestra, and Pylades was proverbial, even though there is little in myth or Greek tragedy to convey the strength of that friendship, as Green argues (p. 417). Phyllis has haunted these poems from time to time; here Ovid ends these mentions of her loneliness with her own end.

56 Cf. Sappho – 'an undercurrent of flame comes under my whole skin.'

57 Ovid has this all ways. He movingly urges us that hatred is vile, but pragmatically reminds us that it isn't all that helpful, either. His balancing of love and hate recalls Catullus: 'I love, I hate; perhaps you ask me why. I don't know, but I feel it happening, and it's torture.'

58 Ovid does sneak in some thoughts here on how (not) to recover from loving your actual wife; but the context makes it sound as though she has done enough wrong for the husband – and poet – to make an example of her in Augustan Rome.

59 A note on the Mozley/Goold Loeb text persuasively explores the idea that this is a formal, legal document.

60 A neat unfolding of two lines from the start of *Art*: 'pick someone you can tell, "Just you I love"' (42) and 'Whatever the world has, you'll find it here' (56). The idea of plenty survives; the uniqueness doesn't.

61 We know this from *Art* 3.292, where we learn that 'they' cry well. There he is talking about women, as if in their absence, in a book supposedly devoted to women. Here he claims to be talking to both men and women (l. 50), but it is not the first time in the poem when the claim seems hollow, even an afterthought.

62 A reference to Philoctetes' bow (see *Cures* III, note 18).

63 Her son, Meleager, would die if a certain log burned.

64 Her husband, Protesilaus, was the first man killed in the Trojan War. She had a sculpture of him made, against her father's wishes. As a result, she burnt herself to death, and rejoined her husband.

65 When his son Palamedes was killed by the Greeks in the Trojan War, Nauplius would avenge his death by luring Greek ships to smash on a promontory.

66 Money isn't a big theme in Euripides' *Hippolytus* (in which the hero, beloved of Phaedra, is dashed against the rocks by Poseidon's bull as a consequence of spurning love); money doesn't feature in many other tragedies, either. Could it be that Ovid is making a joke about the supposed grandeur of Greek tragedy, and gently ribbing Aristotle?

67 Irus the beggar appears in the Odyssey; Hecale is helpful to Theseus.

68 Even in a poem assessing all means of losing love, in which losing love is desirable, even so, Ovid would do anything for (no) love, but he won't do that.

69 Except, we assume, *Cures for Love*.

70 Anacreon composed drinking songs.

71 Noonday sun has also helped the eyes, just as candles have beguiled them in the *Art*; the point is that clear sight will allow you to see faults.

72 The Greek philosopher Heraclitus compared the soul to a fire that drinking would extinguish.

73 Ovid has put his precepts through such a thorough reversal that now even the need to be moderate in all things is under suspicion, just as too much exposure to your mistress can help to cure you. The poet has expressed this with another drinking image at l. 534 above.

TREATMENTS
FOR THE
FEMININE FACE

PREFATORY NOTE

This poem exists as a fragment – clearly two codex sheets of a longer manuscript have survived, which is why we have two disconnected sections of fifty lines each. The first section prepares us for some of the jokes about *couture* and excess that we see in the *Art* Book 3; the second is an extravagantly detailed piece on face-masks.

As Ovid says in the *Art*, this is a short poem that took a lot of work. However elaborate we consider the preparation of these face-packs, the exact nature of the quantities involved gives the poem a convincing air. This is in part parody, drawing attention to some of the absurdities pursued by other didactic poets: for example, Nicander's *Alexipharmaca*, which advises on how to survive a snakebite. But it is just as likely to be practical. I see the poem as halfway between Douglas Dunn's poem 'Ratatouille', which provides a perfectly good recipe, and the rhyming Formula 86 Delayed Action Mouse-Maker in Roald Dahl's *The Witches*.

TREATMENTS FOR THE
FEMININE FACE

1   Learn how to make the best out of your face
    and, girls, what methods will protect your grace.
    It's cultivation that demands we beat
    the brambles back, fill barren soil with wheat.¹

5   It shows us how to sweeten fruit by craft;
    it's how a split tree can accept a graft.
    Culture delights: gold lines a lofty ceiling;
    marble stands on the black land it's concealing.
    Wool's often dipped in tubs of dye from Tyre;

10 ivory's turned to objects of desire.
    The Sabine girls preferred to cultivate
    land rather than themselves; they pressed their
        weight
    on high seats (this was under Tatius' reign)
    and spun, their hardy thumbs taking the strain;

15 they'd pen the lambs their daughters sent to graze
    and put their own logs on the fireplace.
    But you are gentler than your dams of old:
    you want to wear garments woven with gold;
    to mix the scents with which you douse your locks

20 and make your hands conspicuous with rocks.
    Your necks bear stones dug from some eastern clime
    so big few ears can lug two at a time.

But why not strive to please? It's no disgrace,
given that men are so well-groomed these days.
25   The man's so smooth, his bride must find out
    what
accessories he's not already got.
Women dress for themselves, not to be seen
by lovers. Still, no harm in keeping clean.
Deep in the countryside, they fix their hair;
30   hiding on Athos, still they'd take great care.
The pleasure of self-pleasing is well-known:
the look that warms a maiden's heart's her own.
The peacock's feathers rightly win men's praise,
and many other birds will flaunt their grace.
35   This is the way that love exerts its pull,
rather than herbs dread sorceresses cull.
Don't trust grasses, and don't trust blended
    juice,
Nor noxious fluids mares on heat produce;
a Marsian spell can't split a snake in two,
40   and flowing to its source, no wave can do;
and nobody who gives copper a whack
will ever shake the moon out of its track.

Girls, put behaviour in pride of place –
a pleasant nature helps a pleasant face.
45   Love of good manners stays; beauty is blighted
and wrinkles plough a face that once delighted.
When seeing your reflection leaves you flat,
you'll get more wrinkles just because of that.

Integrity endures for many a day.
50 If love depends on that, then it will stay.

*

Here is a way to make complexions gleam
when sleep's dismissed your body from its dream.
The best protection is a facial mask
of Libyan barley shaken from its husk.
55 Measure two pounds of this, to be combined
with two more pounds of vetch, which ten eggs
  bind.[2]
When this has dried upon the passing wind,
then give it to a stubborn ass to grind.
Pound into this two ounces of the shed
60 horn of a hart (the first off from his head).
Once this blends with the powder, then retrieve
the mixture as it passes through a sieve.
Add twelve narcissus bulbs, without skins, and
upon a marble top, squish them by hand.
65 A pound and a half of honey should be dealt
with two ounces of gum, and two of spelt.
Whoever uses that for her complexion
will beam more brightly than her own reflection.
Or for another peel, why don't you try
70 pale lupin seeds? Give gassy beans a fry.
Divide them equally: 12lb in all,
then use black millstones till they're powdered
  small.

You'll need red nitre's foam; also white lead
and iris, grown in an Illyrian bed.
75   Youth's arms should thrash these in equal amounts;
each ground ingredient should weigh 1oz.
One treatment comes from noisy nests: apply
kingfisher cream, and wave your spots goodbye.
Ask me how much, and I won't hesitate
80   to call ½ of an ounce the perfect weight,
and so that you can smear it on your skin
find honey – golden, Greek – and blend it in.
Though incense is what angry gods require,
don't put it all upon the altar's fire.
85   The nitre that you'll use against a growth
mixes with it. Weigh 4oz of both.
Take 9oz of gum, which you should stir
together with a medium cube of myrrh.
When this is pounded up, then sift it through
90   a mesh; to give it bulk, add honey, too.
Results from adding fennel have been fine
(five fennel scruples to the myrtle's nine),
and frankincense, and salt from Libya, and
as much dried rose-leaf as can fit your hand.
95   Pour barley water. Weigh the salt and rose,
and now incense's weight should balance those.
Before long, you must wipe the pack away
from your soft face; the colour, though, will stay.
I saw a girl pick poppies, which she'd mix
100   with fresh water, and rub them on her cheeks.

NOTES

[1] These agricultural images are going in all directions: although they are both here as foils to the virtues of civilisation, the brambles also evoke the encroachments of time, hence age, and the sowing metaphor is even less ambiguous.

[2] If you *are* trying this at home, remember that the Roman pound has 12 ounces.

www.vintage-classics.info